THIRD EDITION

ANTHOLOGY OF SCORES FOR

A History of *Music* in Western Culture

VOLUME TWO: The Classical Era through the Present

Mark Evan Bonds

Department of Music
University of North Carolina at Chapel Hill

Richard Kassel
Editor, Third Edition

D0209632

Prentice Hall
Upper Saddle River   London   Singapore
Toronto   Tokyo   Sydney   Hong Kong   Mexico City

Editor-in-Chief: *Sarah Touborg*
Executive Editor: *Richard Carlin*
Project Manager: *Sarah Holle*
Editorial Assistant: *Emma Gibbons*
Director of Marketing: *Tim Stookesberry*
Senior Marketing Manager: *Kate Mitchell*
Marketing Assistant: *Jennifer Lang*
Senior Managing Editor: *Mary Rottino*
Production Editor: *Macmillan Publishing Solutions/Teresa Christie*

Project Management Liaison: *Joe Scordato*
Senior Operations Supervisor: *Brian Mackey*
Senior Art Director: *Pat Smythe*
Interior and Cover Designer: *Laura Gardner*
Composition: *Macmillan Publishing Solutions*
Full-Service Management: *Macmillan Publishing Solutions*
Printer/Binder: *The Courier Companies*
Cover Printer: *Phoenix Color Corp.*

This book was set in 9/11 Times Roman by Macmillan Publishing Solutions and was printed and bound by The Courier Companies. The cover was printed by Phoenix Color Corp.

Credits and acknowledgments borrowed from other sources and reproduced, with permission, in this textbook appear on pages 612–614.

Library of Congress Cataloging-in-Publication Data

Bonds, Mark Evan.
    A history of music in Western culture : combined volume / Mark Evan Bonds. -- 3rd ed.
        p. cm.
    Includes bibliographical references and index.
    ISBN 0-205-66172-6 (v. 1 : paper) -- ISBN 0-205-66173-4 (v. 2 : paper) --
ISBN 0-205-64531-3 (combined : paper)
    1. Music--History and criticism. I. Title.
    ML160.B75 2009
    780.9--dc22

                                                                2008041660

10   9   8   7   6   5   4   3   2

Prentice Hall
is an imprint of

www.pearsonhighered.com

ISBN 10: 0-205-65699-4
ISBN 13: 978-0-205-65699-8

CONTENTS

99   Symphony in B Major, first movement
(ca. 1740)

Georg Matthias Monn (1717–1750)

CD7, Track 1
Book p. 307

1:32.55

Note: The keyboard part (cembalo) represents the editor's realization of the original figured bass.

2:13.0

Monn's Symphony in B Major exhibits elements of both Baroque and Classical styles. The repetition of the opening four-measure phrase creates a kind of antiphonal effect, and the sequential writing that follows (m. 9) is typical of the Baroque. The bass line, however, is decidedly un-Baroque, in that it provides harmonic underpinning but very little in the way of an independent voice. With its steady drum-like rhythm and repetition of single notes for up to two measures, the bass line also helps create a relatively slow harmonic rhythm.

Formally, the movement represents an early manifestation of sonata form. The exposition (m. 1–31) sets out two different themes in the tonic (1P and 2P, the latter beginning in m. 9), another within the transition from the tonic to the secondary key area (T, beginning in m. 19), and another (1S, m. 26) in the secondary key area, F# major, the dominant of B. The development (m. 32–58) begins with 1P but now in the dominant. The development then circulates through a series of harmonies, none of which establishes an area of clear stability. From m. 39 until the end of the development, a variant of the musical idea 2P predominates. At m. 59, the recapitulation begins with the return of the opening theme (1P) in its original key. At m. 67 we hear what is recognizably 2P, but in a different form. Beginning in m. 79, we hear a variant of the transitional theme (T), which now remains in the tonic, leading to a restatement of 1S (m. 86), likewise in the tonic. The movement ends with the recapitulation and has no coda.

The first movement of Monn's Symphony in B Major.

Section	Exposition					Development		Recapitulation			
Themes	‖:1P	2P	T	1S	:‖:	1P	2P	1P	2P	T	1S :‖
Measure	1	9	19	26		32	39	59	67	79	86
Key	I			V		V	ii (unstable)	I			

Sonata in D Major, K. 492 (ca. 1750?)

Domenico Scarlatti (1685–1757)

CD7, Track 2

Book p. 307

0:19.8

0:37.57

1:54.42

Not all binary form movements from the middle of the 18th century bear the hallmarks of sonata form. Most of Domenico Scarlatti's one-movement sonatas for keyboard, for example, lack a clear recapitulation. The Sonata in D Major, K. 492, features two areas of harmonic stability (tonic and dominant) in the first reprise but lacks a clear return of the opening idea in the tonic within the second reprise. The material originally presented in the dominant, however, is restated in the tonic in the second reprise, beginning in m. 91.

Like the first movement of Monn's Symphony in B Major, Scarlatti's sonata features mixed elements of Baroque and Classical styles. The periodic phrase structure, relatively slow harmonic rhythm, and transparent textures look forward, while the virtuosic runs (m. 36–42, 91–97) and sequential passages (m. 10–16, 36–42, etc.) are more characteristic of the earlier part of the 18th century.

2:16.1   2:33.86

101 Symphony in D Major, Op. 3, No. 2,
first movement (ca. 1752–1755)

Johann Stamitz (1717–1757)

CD7, Track 3
Book p. 308

0:35.23

*) Timpani, Clarini und Oboi fehlen in der Pariser Ausgabe. Der erste Satz ist mit Allegro comodo bezeichnet. Bässe und Viola haben Takt 5–12 und in den Parallelstellen ausgehaltene Töne statt der Achtel.

Note: The keyboard reduction (Klavierauszug) is for rehearsal purposes only and is not part of Stamitz's original score.

0:52.75

1:16.7

*) Die Pariser Druckausgabe (ohne Oboi) giebt auch hier die Melodie der 1. Violine (vgl. die kleinen Noten).

2:05.8

2:29.8

Binary form is not the only historical antecedent to sonata form. Another is the ritornello structure of the typical Baroque aria or concerto. Like sonata form, the ritornello structure features a modulation from a primary to a secondary key area, followed by a period of harmonic instability and a return to the tonic at the end. Thus the first movement of Stamitz's Symphony in D Major, Op. 3, No. 2, although it more closely follows a ritornello structure, can also be analyzed in terms of sonata form. Consistent with ritornello structure, two statements of the opening theme in the tonic (m. 5, m. 103) flank a middle statement of the same theme in the dominant (m. 53), with contrasting material in between. Following the pattern of sonata form, the opening section of the movement progresses from tonic to dominant; the music then moves to a different key area (m. 77) before returning to the tonic (m. 87). The return of the opening theme (m. 103) does not coincide with the return of the tonic, however, and in this sense, the recapitulation is diffused. Many movements from the mid-18th century feature such mixed elements of old (ritornello) and new (sonata) forms, however. Even in the later decades of the 18th century, composers frequently departed from the standard conventions of sonata form.

The relationship of ritornello structure and sonata form in the first movement of Stamitz's Symphony in D Major, Op. 3, No 2.

Ritornello Structure	Ritornello I		Ritornello II		Ritornello III
Sonata form	"Exposition"		"Development"		"Recapitulation"
Themes	1P 2P 1T 2T 1S 2S		1P 2P 2T 1S 2S		1P 2P
Measure	5 13 18 29 37 44		53 61 77 87 94		103 111
Key	I V		V (IV-V) I		

102 Sonata in D Major, Op. 5, No. 2, first movement (1766)
Johann Christian Bach (1735–1782)

CD7, Track 4
Book p. 308

This material is reprinted from J.C. Bach, *Twelve Keyboard Sonatas*, Set 1 (Opus V), Oxford University Press.

0:14.5

0:32.0

2:29.85

No. 102 J. C. Bach: Sonata in D Major, Op. 5, No. 2   ■ 11

3:23.17

3:49.78

By the 1760s, sonata form had established itself as the structural framework for the first movements of most instrumental works, and for some slow movements and many finales as well. Except for concertos, the influence of ritornello structure had largely disappeared. The opening movement of Johann Christian Bach's Keyboard Sonata in D Major, Op. 5, No. 2, first published in 1766, is typical for its time, and not just from the standpoint of form. The simple, straightforward melodies, textures, and rhythms create a movement that is unpretentious in the best sense of the word. The first movement of this sonata offered what 18th-century critics perceived to be a natural form of expression that was unforced, without overt displays of contrapuntal, rhythmic, or textural artifice.

The sharp contrast between this movement by J. C. Bach and a work like his father Johann Sebastian Bach's "Goldberg" Variations, written only 25 years earlier, illustrates the generation gap that divided Classical from Baroque style. In the opening air of the "Goldberg" Variations, the theme is in the bass and remains there through all subsequent variations, while the melody in the soprano is of only momentary significance. In the opening measures of the son's work, in contrast, the lowest voice consists of repeated figurations on a series of triadic harmonies. This Alberti bass—so called because it was a favorite device of an otherwise obscure Italian composer named Domenico Alberti (1710–ca. 1740)—provides harmonic support for the melody in the upper voice but is not itself very engaging. The frequent repetition of the same broken chord necessarily leads to a harmonic rhythm slower than that typically found in music from the Baroque era. J. C. Bach's sonata also avoids the kind of sequential repetition so basic to much of his father's music.

Typically for music of the 1760s, the dimensions of J. C. Bach's movement are relatively small. The exposition presents only one theme in the primary key area (1P, m. 1–8), and the transitional theme (T) suggests a move away from the tonic as early as its second measure (with the A♯ in the bass at the end of m. 10) before cadencing clearly on V/V in m. 18. The first theme in the secondary key area (1S, beginning in m. 19) presents a strong contrast to the opening theme, and the exposition as a whole ends with a clearly articulated cadence (m. 42). During the development, the themes appear in fragments. The end of 1S, for example, appears at the beginning of the development in m. 43, and the beginning of T can be heard in m. 48. In m. 60 the harmony reaches what later theorists would call a "point of furthest remove" from the tonic, in this case B minor. The music then gathers itself for a retransition back to the tonic and the opening theme, which arrives with great emphasis at m. 77, the beginning of the recapitulation. In typical sonata form fashion, the themes are presented in the same order as in the exposition, but this time all in the tonic, and with only small variations and embellishments.

Performance notes: The fortepiano recorded here is a modern-day copy of an instrument built by Stein of Vienna in 1786, very similar to the one shown in the illustration textbook on p. 321.

103 Fantasia in C minor (finale of Keyboard Sonata, Wq. 63/6) (1753)
Carl Philipp Emanuel Bach (1714–1788)

CD7, Track 5

Book p. 313

1) The two phrase-marks are printed thus in the source; but possibly they should end and begin one note later, on the C.

Note: The "Harmonic Skeleton" has been added by the editor of the score and is not part of C. P. E. Bach's original composition.

(f)   (g)   (h) *Bebung* (see Intro. p. 3)

2) Thus in the source. The dotted semibreve A in the r.h. is probably *not* a misprint of a dotted minim, but a way of securing a delayed entry of the *p* r.h. phrase that follows.

2:05

2:28

4:16.5

No. 103 C. P. E. Bach: Fantasia in C minor   ■   **15**

By their nature, fantasias follow no conventional pattern. Rather, they reflect the "fantasy" of the composer and/or performer. The typical fantasia thus often features no central musical idea and is instead characterized by a multiplicity of ideas, often linked by rhapsodic, quasi-improvisatory flourishes. At the beginning of Carl Philipp Emanuel Bach's Fantasia in C minor (originally published as the finale to a three-movement keyboard sonata in 1753), we hear a series of broken arpeggios and seemingly aimless passagework. The music conveys a mood of contemplation. Indeed, it struck the poet Heinrich Wilhelm von Gerstenberg as grappling with issues of life and death, inspiring him to set an elaborate text to this music based on the celebrated soliloquy in Shakespeare's *Hamlet* ("To be, or not to be: that is the question…"). Gerstenberg later set a second text to it as well, this one based on the dramatic moment when Socrates drinks poison rather than compromise his ethical principles. One reason for the serious reaction this work provoked is its dramatic trajectory: it begins with a mood of resigned contemplation, becomes agitated, recedes to a lyrical tone (the Largo section), and concludes with agitated force (Allegro moderato).

Like many fantasias of the time, C. P. E. Bach's is full of abrupt changes and unexpected events. It also features long stretches without any bar lines, emphasizing the rhythmic freedom with which it is to be performed. The notated meter at the opening—allegro moderato—seems almost irrelevant. Only in the middle section do we hear a recognizable theme in a recognizable meter; but this proves transitory.

Performance notes: The clavichord, unlike the harpsichord, allows the performer to inflect a note even after striking a key, applying pressure through the finger to create added vibration, an effect not unlike a string player's vibrato. This device, known as *Bebung* (from the German *beben,* meaning "to shake or quiver") is explictly notated through what look like a series of four staccato marks above a single note and is particularly audible in this recording at m. 19–21 of the middle Largo section.

104 **Piano Sonata in C minor,** Hob. XVI:20,
first movement (1771)

Joseph Haydn (1732–1809)

CD7, Track 6

Book p. 319

1:41

7:57.18

Haydn's Sonata in C minor, Hob. XVI:20, published in 1771, reflects the increasing size and complexity of sonata-form movements in the 1770s. Compared to Bach's Sonata in D Major, Op. 5, No. 2, Haydn's sonata is longer, more varied musically and emotionally, and technically more demanding of the performer.

The first eight measures of the sonata also illustrate Haydn's ability to create irregular patterns even within the constraints of periodic phrase structure. The opening two measures present a standard tonic to dominant progression, leading the listener familiar with this kind of pattern to expect the next two measures to lead back from the dominant to the tonic, completing a closed unit. But Haydn delays the half cadence (a cadence on the dominant) by repeating the turning figure sequentially to create an antecedent phrase of four rather than two measures. The next two measures (5–6) reiterate the tonic, but this time in a lower register—register will be a very important compositional element in this movement—and after a surprise flourish in m. 6, the music returns to the tonic in m. 8. This initial point of harmonic and rhythmic closure, however, is not very strong. The composer does not yet want the music to come to a complete stop, so he creates the expectation of continuity by placing the tonic cadence on the third beat of the measure rather than on the downbeat, and also by leaving it harmonically "empty"—that is, as unharmonized octave Cs. We may be at the end of a sentence, Haydn is telling us, or even of a paragraph, but certainly not the end of a chapter or an entire work. In one sense, then, this opening eight-measure unit fulfills all our expectations about melodic and rhythmic structure. The first four measures take us from the tonic to the dominant, and the second four bring us back to the tonic. Haydn, however, has manipulated the inner workings of this larger progression in ways that are full of small surprises.

Performance notes: Malcolm Bilson's performance on a fortepiano illustrates the striking difference in sound between the instrument during Haydn's lifetime and the modern-day piano. Bilson plays on an original fortepiano made by the Schantz brothers; we know that Haydn purchased an instrument from this Viennese workshop about 1788. Compared to the modern grand piano, the instrument is smaller in every respect, with a span of about only five octaves and a narrower dynamic range. Yet the fortepiano features a lighter mechanism and a more transparent sound: what it lacks in power it makes up for in finesse, and many players today prefer this kind of instrument for repertory of the late 18th and early 19th centuries.

105 String Quartet in C Major, Op. 33, No. 3 (1781)
Haydn

0:33

1:20

3:40

4:58

5:18

6:37

1:44

2:12

4:28.2

4:52

0:34   0:56.5   1:23

1:40

2:06

*) Besser e¹?

The first movement of Haydn's String Quartet in C Major, Op. 33, No. 3 illustrates the characteristic textural richness of his quartets. The repeated notes in the second violin and viola parts in the opening measures seem at first to be preparing us for the entry of a more engaging melodic line, which does indeed begin to emerge in the first violin in m. 2. Yet the surprising changes of pitch in this seemingly innocuous pulsing figure give it a growing significance: the C and E in the opening measures shift to F and D in m. 7, and B♭ and D in m. 13. What appears to be a subordinate figure, completely static in its pitch and rhythm, gradually emerges as a motivic idea in its own right, blurring the boundary between melody and accompaniment. That boundary is similarly ambiguous in the interaction between the first violin and the cello from m. 18 to 26. Are the two parts exchanging the melody from measure to measure, or is the cello figure merely accompanying the longer note values of the violin's melody? What these examples illustrate is the truly obligatory nature of the obbligato accompaniment in this quartet. Blending counterpoint with homophony, Haydn has created a texture in which accompaniment and melody are inextricably linked.

The lively second movement of this quartet, which Haydn labeled "scherzo," follows the typical structure of a minuet, with m. 1–34 constituting the minuet proper; m. 35 to 51 make up the trio. (Why Haydn chose to call this movement and its counterparts in the other quartets in Op. 33 scherzos rather than minuets is not clear; he returned to the designation "minuet" in his later quartets.)

The slow third movement is a sonata form with varied reprise. In this variant of sonata form, the exposition is not repeated note for note, but instead written out and changed in subtle ways. The varied reprise in this particular movement begins with the return to the tonic in m. 30 and a restatement of the opening theme with new melodic embellishments, especially in the first violin. The modulation to the dominant, confirmed in m. 14 in the first statement of the exposition, is repeated in the second statement in m. 43, again with an elaboration in the first violin part. The effect is similar to that of a da capo aria, in which the singer was expected to embellish a reprise the second time through. In this case, however, Haydn specified the embellishments rather than leaving them up to the performer. After a short development section (m. 59–64), the music returns to the tonic (m. 65) at the onset of the recapitulation, which repeats the themes of the exposition, but this time all in the tonic.

The last movement, a rondo, illustrates one of Haydn's favorite devices in this form—to incorporate thematic material from the opening refrain (the A section) within a contrasting episode. The A section (m. 1–22) and the B section (m. 23–26) are clearly distinct. The material in m. 37 to 72, however, which leads back to a second statement of A, is as long as the A and B sections combined and is based on material from A. By manipulating harmonies and fragmenting the thematic material into increasingly small units, Haydn makes the return to A at m. 72 a significant event even though it offers no thematic contrast to what precedes it. What, then, is the formal status of the material in m. 37–72? Because it is based on thematic material from A, it could be considered a statement of A within a typical rondo structure. Functionally, however, it is more like an extended retransition—a return to the opening idea—or even (in sonata-form terms) a development section.

106 Symphony No. 103 in E♭ Major,
first movement (1795)
Haydn

CD7, Track 11

Book p. 328

1:08

29

3:22.15

3:50.75

5:25.25

SP CP

cm   GM:
plagal

Dies Irae

5:51

7:27.35

7:39.9

The powerful, sudden, and wholly unexpected drumroll that opens Haydn's Symphony No. 103 in E♭ Major illustrates what critics of his time had in mind when they wrote of the sublime in music. It would have struck contemporary listeners as loud, bizarre, and portentous—surely a signal announcing some great event—but what kind of event? It gets our attention but not necessarily our sympathy. The musical idea that follows is dark, fragmented, and difficult to grasp, like a painting of a scene shrouded in mist. Only later will we realize that what we are hearing at this point is a premonition of themes to come.

The opening theme in the low strings reinforces the mysterious air of this slow introduction. The first two measures sound very much like the opening of the *Dies irae* ("Day of wrath") from the plainchant Mass for the Dead (see Example 12-2 in the Textbook, p. 329). The slow introduction ends with a curious insistence on the notes G and A♭ (m. 35–39). But what sounds dark and ominous at the end of the slow introduction is immediately transformed into a bright and airy theme at the beginning of the Allegro con spirito that follows. Progressions like this—from somber to bright, dark to light, obscurity to clarity—are another manifestation of what 18th-century critics considered sublime. The sudden deflection from the dominant of C minor to E♭ Major is likewise another portent of things to come, this time of the many other sudden and unexpected modulations that abound in this sonata-form first movement, not to mention the unexpected return of the slow movement's opening in the coda of the first movement at m. 202.

107 Piano Concerto in D Major, K. 107, No. 1, first movement (1772)
Wolfgang Amadeus Mozart (1756–1791)

CD7, Track 12
Book p. 334

*) Zu Entstehungszeit und -ort vgl. Vorwort, S. XVII f.
**) Zum Begriff des „Basso" vgl. Vorwort, S. XIX.
***) Vgl. Vorwort, S. XIX. — Klavierstimme und Generalbaß-Bezifferung sind durchweg von Leopold Mozart geschrieben; hierüber sowie über den etwaigen weiteren Anteil Leopolds im Originalmanuskript vgl. Vorwort, S. XVII f.

0:15.26

0:29.7   0:42.55   0:51.72

No. 107 Mozart: Piano Concerto in D Major, K. 107, No. 1   ■   39

1:24.52

2:06.3

*) Diese Ausführung auch in den folgenden Takten (vgl. Takt 88 ff., Violine I, II).

3:11.68

3:39.4

*) Zur originalen Notierung der Takte 147 f. im Klavier vgl. Krit. Bericht.

4:21.7

The first movement of this concerto is based on the opening movement of Johann Christian Bach's Keyboard Sonata in D Major, Op. 5, No. 2 (Anthology 2/102). Mozart's reworking of this movement illustrates the relationship between sonata form and double-exposition concerto form. For the first eight measures, Mozart closely follows Bach's sonata, adding additional accompaniment in the inner voices (second violins and violas) but making no structural changes. At the beginning of the transition (m. 9), however, when the sonata modulates to the dominant, the concerto stays in the tonic. Mozart then abbreviates much of what J. C. Bach had presented in the secondary key area, adding a cadential figure of his own (m. 24–28) to close out the tutti exposition. All this time the soloist has been playing as a member of the basso continuo, filling in harmonies according to Mozart's figured bass.

The soloist assumes an altogether different function in the solo exposition, which begins at m. 29. Now the melody moves to the piano, the accompaniment moves to the strings, and the basso continuo drops out altogether. In the solo exposition Mozart also follows J. C. Bach's sonata much more closely, modulating to the dominant on the transitional theme (m. 37–46) and staying there to introduce all the themes J. C. Bach had presented in the secondary key area. (In retrospect, we can now see why Mozart abbreviated the tutti exposition: the music would have stayed in the tonic for far too long in proportion to the movement as a whole.)

The first movement of this concerto can also be analyzed in terms of ritornello structure, a form that Mozart never wholly abandoned in his concertos. As in a Baroque concerto, the movement as a whole consists of alternating tutti and solo sections. The contrasting tutti and solo sections are easy to identify in the score with a quick look at the keyboard part: figured bass notation—indicating that the solo instrument is acting as part of the basso continuo—signals a tutti section; the absence of figured bass notation signals a solo section.

108 Piano Concerto in E♭ Major, K. 271,
first movement (1777)
Mozart

CD8, Track 1
Book p. 335

*) Fagott/Bassoon ad lib.

0:42.47

1:31.75

2:28.9

3:48.25

4:11.1

5:31.16

6:03.5

7:41.7

8:15.1

I^6_4

9:32.14

The overlapping patterns of double-exposition concerto form and ritornello structure are evident in all of Mozart's concertos, including the Piano Concerto in E♭ Major, K. 271. The very opening of the first movement reminds us (yet again) that composers were constantly playing with conventions, for here the soloist enters quite unexpectedly as a soloist almost at once (m. 2–7) before receding back into the framework of the basso continuo. (The subsequent marking of *tasto solo* indicates that the soloist is to play only the note indicated, not any harmony above it, until the resumption of the figured bass markings in m. 12.)

From a thematic point of view, Mozart's Piano Concerto K. 271 is tightly organized: almost every idea relates in some fashion to the opening theme (see the diagram in the Textbook, p. 336).

Performance notes: This recording uses a relatively small orchestra playing on period instruments. The transparency of the ensemble's sound allows the period fortepiano to stand out with special clarity, even in those passages in which the keyboard player functions as a member of the basso continuo. Mozart notated two cadenzas for this first movement; the soloist here has chosen the second of these ("B"). The use of the soft pedal on the fortepiano, operated by a lever underneath the keyboard pushed to the side by the player's knee, is particularly evident at m. 17–28 within this cadenza.

109 La serva padrona: "Lo conosco a quegl'occhietti" (1733)
Giovanni Battista Pergolesi (1710–1736)

CD8, Track 2
Book p. 338

1:23.76

64   ■   No. 109 Pergolesi: *La serva padrona*

No. 109 Pergolesi: *La serva padrona*   ■

66 ∎ No. 109 Pergolesi: *La serva padrona*

The origins of opera buffa—comic opera—lie in the tradition of the intermezzo, a work intended for performance between the acts of a larger (serious) opera. Giovanni Battista Pergolesi's intermezzo *La serva padrona* ("The Maidservant as Mistress") was first performed in Naples between the acts of an opera seria also written by Pergolesi. Over time, this intermezzo and others like it became so well known that they were performed alone rather than between the acts of larger works, thus giving rise to opera buffa as a separate genre.

La serva padrona tells the story of a maidservant who, through guile and cunning, becomes mistress of the household in which she had been employed. In contrast to the elaborate cast of characters found in many opere serie of the time, Pergolesi's intermezzo makes do with only two singers, Uberto (a bass), the master of the house, and Serpina (a soprano), the maidservant. (The character of Vespone, a manservant, is entirely mute and limited to mime.) In the duet that closes Act I, "Lo conosco a que gl'occhietti" (I see it in your eyes), Serpina argues that she would be a perfect *padrona* for the lifelong bachelor (who is much less sure of this). The comic nature of their discussion is organized by the principles of phrase structure, featuring the repetition of short simple phrases and single notes that give opera buffa much of its character. The vocal octaves and the more chromatic central section (beginning in m. 28) offer contrast to the otherwise diatonic harmony (in G Major) and predominantly homophonic texture, with frequent unisons in the strings.

Somewhat surprisingly, the orchestra concludes the duet not with its introduction, but with a transposition and expansion of the interlude in measures 55–57. This subverts the ritornello idea common to Baroque music, and reinforces the development of the characters as the duet progresses. Repetition is motivic (very much so), but not at the larger structural level of the da capo aria; many of Mozart's and Rossini's arias are set with similar characterization and psychological progression in mind. The duet points toward the lighter style of the mid-18th century, but also to a less monolithic approach to musical expression.

SERPINA ('little snake')

Lo conosco a quegl' occhietti
Furbi, ladri, malignetti,
Che, sebben voi dite no,
Pur m'accennano di sì.

I know it by your little eyes,
cunning, thievish, wicked eyes,
which, as soon as they say "no,"
nevertheless beckon to me with "yes."

UBERTO

Signorina, v'ingannate.
Troppo in alto voi volate,
Gli occhi ed io dicon no,
Ed è un sogno questo sì.

Madam, you err.
You want to fly too high,
My eyes and I say "no,"
And it's a dream, this "yes."

SERPINA

Ma perché? Non son io bella,
Graziosa e spiritosa?
Su, mirate, leggiadria,
Ve' che brio, che maestà.

But why? Am I not beautiful,
graceful, and spirited?
Here, take aim at this beauty,
See what liveliness, what dignity.

UBERTO

(Ah! costei mi va tentando;
Quanto va che me la fa.)

(Ah! she tempts me;
she makes me do so much.)

SERPINA

(Ei mi par che va calando.)
Via, signore.

(He seems be getting warmer.)
Well, sir.

UBERTO

Eh! vanne via.

Oh! Be gone.

SERPINA

Risolvete.

Make up your mind.

UBERTO

Eh! Matta sei.

Oh! you're crazy.

SERPINA

Son per voi gli affetti miei
E dovrete sposar me.

My feeling are for you,
And you must marry me.

UBERTO

Oh che imbroglio egli è per me!

Oh, what a mess this is for me!

110 Alceste, Act II, Scene 3 (excerpt) (1767; revised 1776)

Christoph Willibald Gluck (1714–1787)

CD8, Track 3
Book p. 342

2:11

3:06

74 ■ No. 110 Gluck: *Alceste*

4:35

6:03

ADMÈTE
Tu m'aimes, je t'adore,
et tu remplis mon cœur des plus vives alarmes.

ALCESTE
Ah! Cher époux, pardonne à ma douleur;
je n'ai pu te cacher mes larmes.

ADMÈTE
Et qui les fait couler?

ALCESTE
On t'a dit à quel prix les Dieux ont consenti

de calmer leur colère
et t'ont rendu des jours si tendrement chéris.

ADMÈTE
Connais-tu cet ami, victime volontaire?

ALCESTE
Il n'aurait pu survivre à ton trépas.

ADMÈTE
Nomme-moi ce héros!

ALCESTE
Ne m'interroge pas!

ADMÈTE
Réponds-moi!

ALCESTE
Je ne puis!

ADMÈTE
Tu ne peux?

ALCESTE
Quel martyre!

ADMÈTE
Explique-toi!

ALCESTE
Tout mon cœur se déchire.

ADMÈTE
Alceste!

ALCESTE
Je frémis!

ADMÈTE
Alceste, au nom des Dieux,
au nom de cet amour si tendre, si fidèle,

ADMETUS
You love me, I adore you
Yet you fill my heart with the greatest anxiety.

ALCESTE
Ah, my husband, pardon my anguish,
Which I can no longer conceal.

ADMETUS
Why do you weep?

ALCESTE
You have heard the sacrifice demanded by the
gods
to calm their anger
So that you may return to your cherished life.

ADMETUS
Do you then know the friend who has
volunteered?

ALCESTE
That person could never have survived your
death.

ADMETUS
Name the noble friend!

ALCESTE
Do not ask!

ADMETUS
Respond!

ALCESTE
I cannot!

ADMETUS
You cannot?

ALCESTE (aside)
What pains!

ADMETUS
Speak!

ALCESTE (aside)
My heart aches!

ADMETUS
Alceste!

ALCESTE (aside)
I tremble!

ADMETUS
Alceste, in the name of the gods, listen to me:
In the name of the tender, faithful love

qui fait tout mon bonheur, qui comble tous mes
vœux:
Romps ce silence odieux,
dissipe ma frayeur mortelle!

ALCESTE
Mon cher Admète, hélas!

ADMÈTE
Tu me glaces d'effroi;
parle! Quel est celui
dont la pitié cruelle l'entraîne à s'immoler pour
moi?

ALCESTE
Peux-tu le demander?

ADMÈTE
O silence funeste!
Parle enfin, je l'exige!

ALCESTE
Eh! Quelle autre qu'Alceste
devait mourir pour toi?

ADMÈTE
Toi? Ciel! Alceste!

[CHOEUR]
O Dieux!

[CHOEUR]
O malheureux Admète,
que poursuit le sort en courroux!
O généreux effort
d'une vertu parfaite!
Alceste meurt pour son époux.

ADMÈTE
O coup affreux!

ALCESTE
Admète!

ADMÈTE
Ah! Laisse-moi, cruelle! Laisse-moi!

ALCESTE
Cher époux!

ADMÈTE
Non, laisse-moi mourir!
Laisse-moi succomber à ma douleur mortelle,
à des tourments que je ne puis souffrir.

That gives me all my happiness, answers all my
prayers:
Say but a word,
And then my mortal terror shall disappear!

ALCESTE
My dear Admetus, alas!

ADMETUS
You fill me with terror!
Speak! Who is the one
Who with cruel pity
Would sacrifice himself for me?

ALCESTE
Can you ask?

ADMETUS
Oh deadly silence!
Speak, I command it!

ALCESTE
Who other than Alceste
Could die for you?

ADMETUS
You? Heavens! Alceste!

[CHORUS]
O gods!

[CHORUS]
Woe to Admetus,
Your fate is pain and torment!
Oh noble gesture
Of perfect virtue!
Alceste dies for her spouse.

ADMETUS
Oh dreadful blow!

ALCESTE
Admetus!

ADMETUS
Ah! Leave me, cruel one, leave me!

ALCESTE
Dear husband!

ADMETUS
No, let me die!
Let me die of mortal pain,
Of torments I cannot bear.

ALCESTE
Calme cette douleur, ce désespoir extrême.
Vis! Conserve des jours si cher à mon amour.

ADMÈTE
Tu veux mourir, tu veux
me quitter sans retour?
Et tu veux que je vive? Et tu dis que tu m'aimes!
Qui t'a donné le droit de disposer de toi?
Les serments de l'Amour et ceux de l'Hymenée,
ne te
tiennent-ils pas à mes loix enchaînée?
Tes jours, tous tes moments ne sont-ils pas à moi?
Peux-tu me les ravir, sans être criminelle?
Peux-tu vouloir mourir, cruelle,
sans trahir tes serments, ton époux et ta foi?

Et les Dieux souffriraient cet affreux sacrifice?

ALCESTE
Ils ont été sensibles à mes pleurs.

ADMÈTE
D'un amour insensé leur barbare caprice
approuverait-il les fureurs?
Non, je cours réclamer leur suprème justice:
Ils tourneront sur moi leurs coups!
Ils reprendront leur première victime,
ou ma main, ne suivant qu'un transport légitime,
satisfera doublement leur courroux.

ALCESTE
Arrête, ô Ciel!
Ah, cher époux!

ADMÈTE
Barbare!
Non, sans toi je ne puis vivre;
tu le sais, tu n'en doutes pas,
Et pour sauver mes jour,
ta tendresse me livre à des maux plus
cruels cent fois que le trépas.
La mort est le seul bien qui me reste à prétendre,
elle est mon seul recours dans mes tourments
affreux,
et l'unique faveur que j'ose encore attendre
de l'équité des Dieux.

ALCESTE
Ah, cher époux.

ADMÈTE
Je ne puis vivre, tu le sais,
tu n'en doutes pas!

ALCESTE
Calm your anguish, this extreme despair.
Live! Preserve this life so dear to my love.

ADMETUS
You wish to die, to leave me,
Never to return?
So that I can live, do you call that love?
Who gave you the right to choose death?
Do not the pledges and oaths of love and marriage

Keep you bound to me?
Do the days of your life belong to you alone?
Can you lawfully take them from me?
Can you wish to die, cruel one,
Without betraying your oaths, your spouse, and
your loyalty?
And could the gods tolerate this terrible sacrifice?

ALCESTE
They have been moved by my tears.

ADMETUS
Could their barbarous capriciousness approve the
frenzies of an insane love?
No, I shall pursue their supreme justice;
They shall redirect their blows toward me;
They shall reclaim their original victim,
Or my own hand, following a rightful path,
Shall doubly satisfy their wrath.

ALCESTE
Stop, oh heavens!
Oh my husband!

ADMETUS
Barbarous one!
No, without you I cannot live,
You know it, you cannot doubt it.
And to save me,
Your tenderness brings me misfortunes,
A hundred times worse than death.
Death is the only good that remains for me,
It is my only recourse in my horrible torments,

And the only grace I can dare attain
From the justice of the gods.

ALCESTE
Ah, dear husband!

ADMETUS
I cannot live, you know it,
You cannot doubt it.

In *Alceste,* Gluck sought to create an opera that was more faithful to the principles of drama than to the demands of singers. This meant pruning away virtuosic passages, eliminating da capo arias (with their embellished repeats and textual repetition), diminishing the distinction between aria and recitative in general, and giving greater prominence to the chorus, as in the dramas of ancient Greece.

The subject-matter of the libretto of *Alceste* is very much in the tradition of opera seria. The story is based on a Greek legend revolving around Queen Alceste's extraordinary devotion to her husband, King Admetus. When the dying Admetus learns from an oracle that he will be saved if another mortal agrees to die in his place, Alceste resolves to sacrifice herself for him. Admetus recovers and Alceste is summoned to the underworld, but Hercules, with the blessing of Apollo, brings her back and she is restored to life.

In this excerpt, Admetus learns that Alceste is the one who will die for him and he pleads with her to change her mind. Here, Gluck skillfully weaves together accompanied recitative, chorus, aria, and duet into a musically continuous dramatic sequence:

- *Accompanied recitative* (m. 486–524). In the opening dialogue, Admète (French for Admetus) pleads with Alceste to reveal who has agreed to die for him. She resists but in the end admits that she herself is the victim.

- *Chorus* (m. 525–538). At the climactic moment when Alceste reveals that she is to be the sacrificial victim, the Chorus interjects with an outcry of "O Dieux!" ("O ye gods!"). This is in keeping with principles of ancient Greek tragedy, in which the chorus reflects the perspective of the community as a whole, transcending that of any individual character. After Admète registers his own astonishment, the chorus sings a lament for Admète and praises Alceste for her courage and love toward her husband.

- *Accompanied recitative* (m. 538–590). The dialogue resumes. Admète admonishes Alceste, telling her that she will be breaking her marriage vows by abandoning him if she dies and leaves him alone. He calls on the gods to intercede. Alceste answers these protestations calmly, ending the dialogue (in m. 589–590) with the pleading phrase *Ah, cher époux* ("Ah, dear husband").

- *Aria* (m. 591–638). Without fanfare or ritornello, the accompanied recitative flows into an aria, sung by Admète, who proclaims his love for Alceste and tells her that he cannot live without her. The aria adheres to no conventional structure, following instead to the sense of the text. In m. 623, for example, when Admète declares that death is his only salvation, the music shifts abruptly from andante and 3/4 time to alla breve presto.

- *Interruption* (m. 638–639). Just before the end of Admète's aria, Alceste interrupts with a simple but dramatic repetition of her earlier plea, *Ah, cher époux.*

- *Return of aria's opening section* (m. 639–644). The tempo shifts to moderato, the meter back to 3/4, and Admète closes by repeating the key phrase from the opening part of his aria just before leaving the stage: *Je ne puis vivre, tu le sais, tu n'en doutes pas* ("I cannot live [without you], you know it, you have no doubt of that").

By returning to earlier material at the end of the aria, Gluck is to some extent following the conventions of the da capo aria, including even the exit convention. But the differences here are more revealing than the similarities: the return is extremely brief, and virtuosity for its own sake plays no role at all. The repetition reinforces the text, reminding us that in spite of Admète's desire to die, his overwhelming emotion is one of grief at the thought of losing Alceste.

III Don Giovanni, K. 527, Act I, Scenes 1–4
(1787)
Mozart

CD8, Track 4

Book p. 345

Note: This is a piano reduction of Mozart's original version for voices and orchestra.

2:35

No. 111 Mozart: *Don Giovanni* ■ **83**

3:03

1:54.22

5:31.5

1:06.5

3:21.33

0:54.38

3:20.73

The plot of *Don Giovanni* is based on the legend of Don Juan, a nobleman and notorious libertine. Lorenzo Da Ponte's libretto is both comic and serious, pitting men against women and nobles against commoners. The title character is at once malevolent and alluring, a man who openly flaunts conventional morality, pursuing instead his own pleasure under the guise of "liberty." At the beginning of the opera he slays the Commendatore (Commandant), the father of Donna Anna, a woman who has just fought off the Don's attempted assault. At the end of the opera, the statue of the Commendatore consigns the unrepentant Don to the flames of Hell.

The overture and first three scenes of *Don Giovanni,* which together constitute some twenty minutes of continuous music and seamless dramatic action, demonstrate the way Mozart integrates buffa and seria elements. True to the principles of Gluck's operatic creed, Mozart uses the overture to set the tone of the opera as a whole, with its unpredictable juxtaposition of tragedy and farce. When the curtain rises we find Leporello, the servant of Don Giovanni, standing guard outside a nobleman's house while his master attempts to seduce yet another woman. Even before Leporello sings a single note, the music announces that he is a commoner: the opening theme, which Leporello picks up when he begins his aria-monologue, bounces back and forth between tonic and dominant. There is nothing sophisticated about this theme. It is harmonically, rhythmically, and melodically simple, almost to the point of simple-mindedness. Leporello is complaining to himself about the wicked ways of his master while at the same time longing to be a "gentleman" himself. With its relentlessly syllabic text underlay and vehement repetitions of "No, no, no," the aria sounds appropriately comical.

But as in the overture, the juxtaposition of comedy and tragedy occurs without warning. Leporello's monologue segues into a frantic duet between two members of an altogether different class: the noblewoman Donna Anna and the nobleman Don Giovanni. Donna Anna pursues the unknown man (Don Giovanni), who attempts to escape unrecognized. Almost at once, the duet becomes a trio as Leporello joins their agitated exchange with more of his melodically simple line, this time commenting on the action and predicting that his master's philandering will bring his own ruin.

A new dramatic unit begins with the arrival of the Commendatore, Donna Anna's father. He demands a duel with the unknown intruder. Don Giovanni reluctantly accepts, and deals the Commendatore a mortal wound. Again, Leporello comments on the scene as it transpires before him, this time with an even greater sense of gloom. There follows a brief dialogue in secco recitative between Don Giovanni and Leporello, after which they exit. We then move directly into another dramatic unit, still with no real break in the music. Donna Anna returns, having summoned the aid of her kind-hearted but rather boring fiancé, Don Ottavio. During the accompanied recitative that follows they discover her father's body and she faints. Don Ottavio revives her so efficiently, however, that she is soon able to launch into her part of a powerfully dramatic duet (*Fuggi, crudele, fuggi*) at the end of which they swear together to avenge her father's death. The music, agitated and virtuosic, comes from the world of opera seria. Mozart fuses the reflective power of aria (Donna Anna's shock at the death of her father) with the interchange of duet (Don Ottavio's promise of consolation and revenge), all interrupted at unpredictable moments by powerful outbursts of accompanied recitative.

Clearly, Mozart wanted to create a sense of dramatic continuity for the entire opening sequence of events, for it is only now, at the end of this extended duet, that he gives the audience its first opportunity to applaud. The arias and ensembles are not, as is so often the case in opera seria, reflections on events that have already happened. On the contrary, they are part of the action, propelling it forward. The events of the drama, in other words, move through the music.

One of the devices Mozart uses to structure this extended series of units is tonality. The sequence begins and ends in D minor, and the choice of key in between is closely coordinated with the drama unfolding on stage. Each dramatic unit has its own distinctive key, different from yet related to the one before and the one after.

The integration of music and drama is evident as well in the two subsequent numbers. The first of these, *Ah, chi mi dice mai* ("Ah, who shall ever tell me"), begins like an aria. Donna Elvira, who had been seduced and abandoned by Don Giovanni long before the curtain has gone up, is asking herself if she will ever again find that "barbarian," promising to "cut out his heart" if she does. Her demanding vocal line, full of large leaps and covering a wide range, signals that she is a noblewoman, a character who would be at home in an opera seria. As she is singing, Don Giovanni and Leporello see her from a distance, and the aria becomes a trio. Don Giovanni does not at first recognize her (a curious reversal from the previous scene in which he escaped unrecognized), and so he is unaware that it is he she is raging about. With another seduction clearly in mind, he steps forward to console her. The moment they recognize each other, the ensemble ends. The music changes without a pause to secco recitative, and the drama presses on. Once again Mozart deprives the audience of an opportunity to applaud. Instead, we watch Donna Elvira's astonishment turn to rage as Don Giovanni slips away, leaving Leporello to deal with her. In his ensuing aria, *Madamina! il catalogo è questo* ("Madam! Here is the catalogue"), Leporello tries to assuage Donna Elvira with evidence that she is "neither the first nor the last" of Don Giovanni's conquests. He shows her a catalogue he has kept of all of Don Giovanni's lovers. In the first part of the aria Leporello enumerates his master's seductions by country; in the second part he describes them by type (old or young, fair-haired or dark-haired, large or small). The music reflects this shift of focus. The first part is allegro; the second part, with its own theme, moves at a more leisurely tempo (Andante con moto).

112 Requiem, K. 626, Introit and Kyrie (1791)
Mozart

CD8, Track 8
Book p. 352

1:17.88

1:52.66

3:07.21

Requiem aeternam dona eis, Domine.
Et lux perpetua luceat eis.
Te decet hymnus, Deus, in Sion,
Et tibi reddetur votum in Jerusalem
Exaudi orationem meam
Ad te omnis caro veniet.

Kyrie eleison.
Christe eleison.
Kyrie eleison.

Rest eternal grant unto them, O Lord.
And may light perpetual shine upon them.
A hymn, Lord, becometh thee in Zion,
And a vow shall be paid to thee in Jerusalem.
Hear my prayer,
To thee all flesh shall come.

Lord, have mercy.
Christ, have mercy.
Lord, have mercy.

113 Die Zauberflöte, Act I: "Der Vogelfänger bin ich ja" (1791)
Mozart

CD8, Track 10

Book p. 355

In their orchestration, melodic style, and demand for vocal virtuosity, the sacred works of Haydn, Mozart, and others are indeed sometimes hard to distinguish from their secular theatrical works. On the whole, however, church music remained relatively conservative during the Classical era, retaining the basso continuo long after it had been abandoned in the concert hall, and well after it was still necessary from a strictly technical point of view. Sacred music also preserved more of the tradition of strict counterpoint than was customary in theater, chamber, or orchestral music.

The Introit of Mozart's unfinished *Requiem,* K. 626, is a good example of the synthesis of older and newer styles often found in the sacred music of the Classical era. For this Adagio, Mozart drew on the opening chorus from Handel's *Funeral Anthem for Queen Caroline,* written in 1737, and available to Mozart in Vienna through Baron Gottfried van Swieten, a nobleman who took a special interest in the works of Handel and J. S. Bach. For the section beginning with the words "Te decet hymnus Deus in Sion" ("To thee, Lord in Zion, we sing a hymn"), Mozart brings in an even older source of sacred music, Gregorian chant. Here, in the soprano, he introduces the Ninth Psalm Tone (see Chapter 1), also associated in German-speaking lands with the Magnificat, another hymn of praise to God. The concluding "Dona eis pacem" ("Grant them peace") section brings back the opening theme ("Requiem aeternam") but now combines it with a new countersubject. The movement ends in the dominant, to be resolved in the Kyrie, which follows without pause.

The manuscript left by Mozart comprises the Kyrie's vocal parts and the basso continuo line; its orchestration, as well as that of other movements (and, in some cases, entire movements), were completed by composer friends of Mozart at the request of his widow, Constanze, so that she could collect the remaining portion of the commission fee. As with the Introit, Mozart based the Kyrie (Allegro) on a Handel work, in this case a fugue from *Messiah* Van Swieten commissioned an orchestration of Handel's oratorio from Mozart that was performed in 1789.) The result is a work of neo-Baroque imitative counterpoint that ends only at the final Adagio, a chordal cadence in the tonic.

84

(pfeift von fern)

(kommt heraus)

1. Der Vo-gel-fän-ger bin ich ja, stets lu-stig hei-ßa hop-sa-sa! Ich Vo-gel-fän-ger
2. Der Vo-gel-fän-ger bin ich ja, stets lu-stig hei-ßa hop-sa-sa! Ich Vo-gel-fän-ger
*)3. Wenn al-le Mädchen wä-ren mein, so tauschte ich brav Zu-cker ein: die, wel-che mir am

*) Die 3. Strophe fehlt sowohl in der Handschrift Mozarts als auch im Erstdruck des Textbuches; sie findet sich erst in späteren Ausgaben, z.B. in einem Druck aus dem Jahre 1795 (ohne Ortsangabe).

85

bin be-kannt bei Alt und Jung im gan-zen Land.
bin be-kannt bei Alt und Jung im gan-zen Land.
lieb-sten wär, der gäb ich gleich den Zu-cker her.

Weiß mit dem Lo-cken
Ein Netz für Mädchen
Und küß-te sie mich

um-zu-gehn und mich aufs Pfei-fen zu ver-stehn.
möch-te ich, ich fing sie du-tzend-weis für mich!
zärt-lich dann, wär sie mein Weib und ich ihr Mann.

(pfeift)

Drum kann ich froh und
Dann sperr-te ich sie
Sie schlief an mei-ner

lu-stig sein, denn al-le Vö-gel sind ja mein.(pfeift)
bei mir ein, und al-le Mädchen wä-ren mein.
Sei-te ein, ich wieg-te wie ein Kind sie ein.

(will nach der Arie nach der Pforte gehen)

Fine

Dal Segno

No. 113 Mozart: *Die Zauberflöte* ■ 111

Der Vogelfänger bin ich ja,
Stets lustig heisa hop-sa-sa!
Ich Vogelfänger bin bekannt
Bei alt und jung im ganzen Land.
Weiß mit dem Lokken umzugehn,
Und mich aufs Pfeiffen zu verstehn!
Drum kann ich froh und lustig sein,
Denn alle Vögel sind ja mein!

Der Vogelfänger bin ich ja,
Stets lustig heisa hop-sa-sa!
Ich Vogelfänger bin bekannt
Bei alt und jung im ganzen Land.
Ein Netz für Mädchen möchte ich,
Ich fing sie dutzendweis für mich!
Dann sperrte ich sie bei mir ein,
Und alle Mädchen wären mein.

Wenn alle Mädchen wären mein
So tauschte ich brav Zucker ein,
Die welche mir am liebsten wär,
Der geb ich gleich den Zucker her,
Und küsste sie mich zärtlich dann,
Wär sie mein Weib und ich ihr Mann.
Sie schlief an meiner Seite ein,
Ich wiegte wie ein Kind sie ein.

Yes, I am the Birdcatcher,
Always merry, heisa, Hop-sa-sa!
I, the birdcatcher, am well known
To old and young throughout the land.
I know how to handle traps
And make myself understood on the pipes!
So I can be happy and merry,
For all the birds indded are mine!

Yes, I am the Birdcatcher,
Always merry, heisa, hop-sa-sa!
I, the birdcatcher, am well known
To old and young throughout the land.
A net for maidens is what I'd like,
I'd catch them by the dozens for me!
Then lock them up with me,
And all the girls would be mine.

If all the girls were mine
I'd barter honestly for sugar,
And I'd give to the girl I liked the best
The sugar right away,
And if she then kissed me tenderly,
She would be my wife and I her husband.
She sleep by my side,
I would cradle her to sleep like a child.

--Transl. MEB

In Die Zauberflöte Mozart portrays two classes of characters to illustrate the serious and comic sides of opera. A fellow Mason, Emanuel Schikaneder (1751–1812), composer, librettist, and actor, offered the "fairy-tale opera" to Mozart, who responded with magnificent arias and duets for his "noble characters"—the future lovers, the benevolent father figure, the demonic mother figure—as they participate in a Masonic philosophical allegory. For the comic side, he focuses primarily on the bird-catcher Papageno (played originally by Schikaneder), who is given the folksiest German-sounding music imaginable, eminently hummable and instantly memorable. Papageno makes his Act I entrance with the strophic aria "Der Vogelfänger bin ich ja" (Yes, I am the bird-catcher), in which he describes his profession and his longing for a spouse. The orchestral accompaniment provides the light-hearted bounce to support the upbeat mood, and "covers" for him by incorporating his panpipe interjections (in the likelihood that having the singer do it himself would be impractical for any number of reasons).

114 Italien (Kennst du das Land) (1795–1796)
Johann Friedrich Reichardt (1752–1814)

CD8, Track 11

Book p. 355

Johann Friedrich Reichardt's "Italien" (Italy) offers a good example of the kind of song writing that flourished throughout the Classical era. The setting is strophic and almost entirely syllabic. Both the vocal and piano parts are straightforward and technically undemanding. The range of the vocal line barely exceeds an octave, and is mostly doubled by the piano. The text, also known as "Kennst du das Land" (Do you know the land), is from Goethe's widely read novel *Wilhelm Meisters Lehrjahre* ("Wilhelm Meister's Years of Apprenticeship"), the story of a young man's coming of age. Wilhelm is an aspiring actor who falls in with an odd assortment of characters, one of whom is a mysterious young girl named Mignon. She has no family, and Wilhelm becomes something of a father figure to her, but there is a powerful erotic tension beneath the surface of their relationship. From time to time throughout the novel, Mignon sings songs, of which Goethe gives only the words. Zelter was one of the first composers to set these texts to music, and Goethe expressed his pleasure with Zelter's settings of his texts. (They even collaborated on some singspiels.) Many later composers were also drawn to this and other texts by Goethe that are not nearly so straightforward.

Kennst du das Land, wo die Zitronen blühn,

Im dunkeln Laub die Goldorangen glühn,
Ein sanfter Wind vom blauen Himmel weht,
Die Myrte still und hoch der Lorbeer steht,
Kennst du es wohl?
Dahin! dahin
Möcht' ich mit dir, o mein Geliebter, ziehn.

Kennst du das Haus? Auf Säulen ruht sein Dach,
Es glänzt der Saal, es schimmert das Gemach,
Und Marmorbilder Stehn und sehn mich an:

Was hat man dir, du armes Kind, getan?
Kennst du es wohl?
Dahin! dahin
Möcht' ich mit dir, o mein Beschützer, ziehn.

Kennst du den Berg und seinen Wolkensteg?
Das Maultier sucht im Nebel seinen Weg;
In Höhlen wohnt der Drachen alte Brut;
Es stürzt der Fels und über ihn die Flut.
Kennst du ihn wohl?
Dahin! dahin
Geht unser Weg! o Vater, lass uns ziehn!

Do you know the land where the lemon trees blossom?
Among dark leaves the golden oranges glow.
A gentle breeze from blue skies drifts.
The myrtle is still, and the laurel stands high.
Do you know it well?
There, there
would I go with you, my beloved,

Do you know the house? On pillars rests its roof.
The great hall glistens, the room shines,
and the marble statues stand and look at me, asking:
"What have they done to you, poor child?"
Do you know it well?
There, there
would I go with you, oh my protector,

Do you know the mountain and its path?
The muletier searches in the clouds for his way;
in the caves dwells the dragon of the old breed.
The cliff falls, and over it the flood.
Do you know it well?
There, there
leads our way; oh father, let us go!

115 Africa (1770, 1778)
William Billings (1746–1800)

Billings, a native of Boston, was one of the first American-born composers to achieve international fame (albeit posthumously). He was largely self-taught, and his musical style, although indebted to English precedents, exhibits a certain roughness that gives it great energy. His hymn "Africa" was printed in his first collection, *The New-England Psalm-Singer* (1770), without text; he later added verses by the great English hymnodist Isaac Watts when it was republished in *The Singing Master's Assistant* (1778). The work's name, "Africa," is an arbitrary designation of the tune itself; Billings and other hymnodists chose geographical names (mostly local towns) for their tunes, and some were later set to new texts. English-language hymns used a small number of metrical patterns: "Africa" is set in common meter (or C. M.), consisting of four lines that alternate in length between eight and six syllables; in this case, Watts rhymed the second and fourth lines only, in the same manner that Emily Dickinson wrote her poetry (other hymns in this meter also rhyme the first and third lines, as in "Amazing Grace"). As with other Billings choruses, the four-part texture is often expanded in performance to six parts by doubling the treble and tenor lines at the octave. The ensemble may also choose to double the vocal parts instrumentally.

Text for additional verses:

2. God on his thirsty Sion-Hill
Some Mercy-Drops has thrown,
And solemn Oaths have bound his Love
To show'r Salvation down.

3. Why do we then indulge our Fears,
Suspicions and Complaints?
Is he a God, and shall his Grace
Grow weary of his saints?

4. Can a kind Woman e'er forget
The Infant of her Womb,
And 'mongst a thousand tender Thoughts
Her Suckling have no Room?

5. Yet, saith the Lord, should Nature change,
And Mothers Monsters prove,
Sion still dwells upon the Heart
Of everlasting Love.

6. Deep on the Palms of both my Hands
I have engrav'd her Name;
My Hands shall raise her ruin'd Walls,
And build her broken Frame.

Performance notes:

Performance notes: In this recording, the Hillier ensemble attempts to recreate what we know of the style of part-singing prevalent in colonial New England, producing a sound that is clear, exuberant, and at times even piercing. Tenors and basses alone sing the first strophe; the sopranos double the tenors at the octave for the second strophe, then sing their own independent line for the third. In the fourth strophe, the altos join in.

116 Lyrical Pieces op. 47: Halling
Edvard Grieg (1843–1907)

CD9, Track 1
Book p. 382

Norway, which had been ruled by Denmark since the 14th century, was caught up in a struggle between Denmark and Sweden associated with the outcome of the Napoleonic wars. In 1814, Norway accepted a union with Sweden that allowed it constitutional and military independence at the price of Swedish hegemony. During the rest of the 19th century, a nationalist cultural movement began to flourish. Its two most famous exponents, the composer Edvard Grieg and the playwright Hendrik Ibsen (1828–1906), collaborated on the verse drama *Peer Gynt* (1867), which premiered in Christiania (now Oslo), Norway, in 1876. The play, on a scale with Goethe's *Faust*, was not originally intended for performance, and it makes great demands on its audiences and actors (six hours in length) as well as designers and producers (five acts and 37 scenes, with one act played entirely in darkness).

Grieg's incidental music has survived, and the best known of the original 23 numbers are found in the two orchestral *Peer Gynt* suites of four movements each (opus 46, 1888; opus 55, 1891). For the most part, the score is composed in the composer's early manner, as yet little touched by the Norwegian folk melodic influence. But two examples of music in Norwegian traditional style set the tone early on: two dance tunes played on the traditional Hardanger fiddle (*hardingfele*), a violin with sympathetic strings and a variety of cross-tunings. One of these dances in duple meter, a "Halling," accompanies difficult, almost acrobatic steps. Heard here in its original version, this is followed by a version for piano (emphasizing the drone) included by Grieg in one of his many sets of *Lyrical Pieces* (opus 47, no. 4, 1885–88).

117 Symphony No. 3 in E♭ Major ("Eroica"), Op. 55 (1803)

Ludwig van Beethoven (1770–1827)

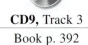

CD9, Track 3

Book p. 392

117a First Movement

full Statement of PT

0:50.26

1:30.95

1:50.39

5:37.74

transition motive

6:49.34

No. 117 Beethoven: Symphony No. 3 in E♭ Major   ■   **121**

7:06.49

7:57.81

9:01.06

10:07

10:40.55

11:40.39

12:10.59

14:21.37

14:46.95

No. 117 Beethoven: Symphony No. 3 in E♭ Major   ■   131

CD9, Track 4
Book p. 392

0:53.21   1:38

"happy remembrance"

Thema III

3:40.04

5:21.07

7:37.42

No. 117 Beethoven: Symphony No. 3 in E♭ Major   ■ **137**

8:30

9:35.58

10:15.89

Beethoven's *Eroica* breaks new ground in many respects. The sonata-form first movement is of an unprecedented length; at 691 measures, it dwarfs any previous sonata-form first movement, and in the slow movement, Beethoven became the first composer to make symphonic use of the march.

First movement: The two loud tonic chords at the opening of the first movement (Allegro con brio) provide the briefest of introductions and serve a double function: to catch the audience's attention and to allow Beethoven to introduce the principal theme at a soft volume. The metrically regular, triadic opening of this theme (m. 3–6) contrasts with its syncopated, chromatic continuation (m. 7–10). The transition section (m. 45–83) is unusually long, occupying roughly 25 percent of the exposition. It contains three distinct thematic ideas, each of which will be developed later in the movement. The first idea in this secondary key area (the dominant, B♭ major), beginning in m. 83, offers a distinct but brief contrast to the turbulence of the opening and the transition. The sense of forward momentum soon returns, however, culminating in a series of syncopated chords (m. 123–131) just before the end of the exposition.

Within the development (m. 152–398), the fugato—a passage that begins like a fugue but does not sustain itself after a series of initial entries—that begins at m. 236 leads to a thematic standstill in a series of loud repeated chords (m. 248–283). Syncopation is emphasized at the expense of melody. The theme beginning in m. 284 that follows these chords is one we have not heard before. The introduction of an entirely new theme in the development of a sonata-form movement was not without precedent—Haydn did it in his *Farewell* Symphony of 1772. Beethoven, however, expands on this device in an innovative way by working his new theme into the remainder of the movement and restating it prominently in the tonic in the coda.

Beethoven has additional surprises in store before the recapitulation. The long passage on the dominant between m. 338 and 358 seems to signal the end of the development section and the beginning of the retransition to the tonic. But Beethoven avoids the tonic and extends the development still further. The true retransition begins at m. 382 with a thinning-out of the orchestral texture over an extended V^9 harmony. Then, in a quiet yet deeply bizarre gesture, Beethoven has a solo horn enter with the opening theme in the tonic (m. 395) while the strings are still sounding a dominant harmony. In effect, Beethoven has deliberately written an apparent mistake into the score, making it seem to an unsuspecting listener that one of the hornists has come in too early.

The recapitulation itself, which begins at m. 398, is highly unstable at first, moving from the tonic to the supertonic (F major) after only eleven measures. The harmony finally settles firmly on the tonic with the full orchestral passage that begins in m. 430. From this point onward, the recapitulation is fairly stable. The coda, which begins in m. 557, is substantial. It amounts, in effect, to a second development section, during which the new theme introduced in m. 284 is finally restated in the tonic (beginning at m. 589).

Second movement: Beethoven's label at the head of the second movement—*Marcia funebre* ("Funeral March")—is in a sense superfluous, because the music itself bears all the characteristic features of a funeral march: minor mode, slow tempo (Adagio assai), the imitation of muffled drums in the double basses, dotted rhythms in the melody, and a subsequent alternation between minor- and major-mode themes. The movement is structured to feature the prominent return of the mournful opening figure (A) at key points (m. 1, 105, 173) between contrasting ideas.

118 Symphonie fantastique, fifth movement (finale) (1830)
Hector Berlioz (1803–1869)

CD9, Track 5

Book p. 401

Si l'on ne peut trouver deux Cloches assez graves pour sonner l'un des trois UT et l'un des trois SOL qui sont écrits, il vaut mieux employer des Pianos. Ils exécuteront alors la partie de Cloche en double octave, comme elle est écrite. (Note de H. Berlioz.)

Kann man nicht zwei Glocken finden, welche gross genug sind, um eines der drei C und eines der drei G, die vorgeschrieben sind, erklingen zu lassen, so ist es besser, die Klaviere zu verwenden. Man spielt dann die Glockenpartie in doppelter Octave, so wie sie geschrieben ist.

If 2 bells are not available which are large enough to produce one of the 3 Cs and one of the 3 Gs as written, it is better to use the pianofortes. In such event the bell-part must be played with double-octaves as written.

1:29

1:47

2:55.75

*) Die Herausgeber empfehlen, die folgenden Takte auf fünfsaitigen Contrabässen in der tiefen Octave zu spielen.
Les mesures suivantes se jouent une octave plus bas sur la contrebasse à 5 cordes. (Note des Éditeurs.)
The editor wishes the following bars to be played on a 5-stringed double-bass in the lower octave.

3:21.15

4:23.38

297

74

306

6:09.68

7:13.51

Dies irae et Ronde du Sabbat (ensemble).
Dies irae and witches' round dance (together).

8:00.62

8:25.28

9:06.17

Berlioz's "Fantastic Symphony" is a deeply autobiographical work. Inspired by the composer's infatuation with an actress named Harriet Smithson, the symphony's prose program narrates the emotional turmoil of a young musician as he falls in love (the first movement), sees her at a ball (second movement), realizes that she may be spurning him (third movement), is executed for murdering her (fourth movement), and then finally sees her in hell, transformed into a witch (fifth movement, the "Dream of a Witches' Sabbath").

Berlioz's prose program for the finale, distributed at the work's premiere, reads as follows:

> Dream of a Witches' Sabbath. He [the artist] sees himself at the Sabbath, in the middle of a frightening troupe of ghosts, sorcerers, monsters of every kind, all gathered for his funeral rites. Strange noises, groans, bursts of laughter, distant cries to which other cries seem to respond. The beloved melody reappears, but it has lost its noble and shy character. It is nothing more than the melody of a common dance, trivial and grotesque; it is she who comes to join the Sabbath . . . A roar of joy at her arrival . . . She throws herself into the diabolical orgy . . . Funeral knell, burlesque parody of the *Dies irae*. Witches' Round Dance. The dance and *Dies irae* combined.

The structure of this finale is appropriately unconventional. After an extended introduction (m. 1–39), we hear what Berlioz himself called a "trivial and grotesque" version of the original *idée fixe* on the E♭ clarinet. In its original form in the first movement, this had been a lyrical, flowing melody played by violins and flutes:

Berlioz, *Symphonie fantastique*, first movement, m. 72–111: the initial appearance of the principal melody.

In the finale, this graceful idea becomes four-square and common. It is followed by a contrasting section based on the *Dies irae* (beginning at m. 127), followed in turn by the "Witches' Round Dance" (beginning at m. 241). In a brief but spectacular display of counterpoint, Berlioz then presents both the Witches' Round Dance and the *Dies Irae* simultaneously (beginning at m. 414).

Berlioz's orchestration is particularly noteworthy in this work. In additon to the standard strings, winds, and percussion, he calls for an orchestra that includes piccolo, English horn, E♭ clarinet, four horns, two cornets, three trombones, two ophicleides (a forerunner of the tuba), a bass drum, a snare drum, cymbals, bells, and two harps. Berlioz also draws sounds out of these instruments that are something less than beautiful. Listen, for example, to the downward flute glissandos at m. 8–9; it is almost as if the instruments (or their players) have lost all energy. The tapping of the strings with the wooden part of the bow (*col legno*, m. 444) is another sonority that strives to create a sensation lying out of the realm of the ordinary.

119 Overture to A Midsummer Night's Dream (1826)
Felix Mendelssohn (1809–1847)

CD9, Track 6
Book p. 406

1:06.60

No. 119 Mendelssohn: *Overture to A Midsummer Night's Dream*　■　173

2:01.31

2:33.36

No. 119 Mendelssohn: *Overture to A Midsummer Night's Dream* ■ **175**

2:55.07

3:43.28

4:35.63

5:16.58

5:54.09

6:54.18

7:47.60

8:48.30

No. 119 Mendelssohn: *Overture to A Midsummer Night's Dream*   ■   **193**

9:16.87

9:54.1

Felix Mendelssohn wrote his *Overture to A Midsummer Night's Dream* when he was 17 years old; only later did he compose additional movements called for within the course of Shakespeare's play. In this sonata-form overture, Mendelssohn presents a succession of themes representing the play's main characters. Measures 1–5, given entirely to the winds, serve as an introduction to the whole and draw us into the enchanted forest that is the setting for much of the play. The scurrying, high-pitched figure in the strings that begins in m. 5 conjures up the kingdom of the fairies, led by Oberon and Titania, whereas the pompous theme that begins at m. 62 suits the human ruler, Theseus. The first theme in the secondary key area (beginning at m. 130) corresponds to the young humans—two women and two men—who over the course of the play, through magic, will fall in and out of love with one another in various combinations. Finally, the exposition's closing theme (beginning at m. 195) can be readily associated with the "rude mechanicals," the artisans who in Shakespeare's comedy present a play-within-a-play. One of these artisans, a weaver named Bottom, appears at one point in the play with the head of an ass, a transformation reflected in the music by an unmistakable braying sound at m. 200 and elsewhere. In the development section (beginning at m. 250), the scurrying theme associated with fairies predominates. One of the ways Mendelssohn captures the sometimes chaotic magical spirit of the midsummer night's forest is through the simultaneous use of disparate dynamics. At m. 294, for example, he brings in the horns *fortissimo*, with the added direction of *con tutta la forza*—"with all force"—even as the strings and high winds maintain their elfin *pianissimo* figure. The dreamy coda (beginning at m. 620) leads us to wonder, as in Shakespeare's play, if all we have witnessed has been real or imagined.

*) Während des ganzen Andantes hat der Klavierspieler ununterbrochen die Verschiebung (una corda) anzuwenden, das Zeichen „🎵." bezieht sich außerdem auf den zeitweisen Gebrauch des gewöhnlichen Pedalzuges.

2:41.09

1:27.51

The second movement of Beethoven's Fourth Piano Concerto, Op. 58, illustrates the kind of dramatic contrast between soloist and orchestra that would become a staple of the 19th-century concerto repertory. The soloist and the orchestra—limited in this movement to the strings—engage in an extended dialogue that moves from confrontation to resolution. The strings open with a loud unison figure characterized by dotted rhythms and staccato articulation. The piano responds with an utterly different kind of statement, a lyrical, hymn-like theme that Beethoven marks *molto cantabile*. To underscore the timbral difference between soloist and orchestra, Beethoven calls on the pianist to play virtually the entire movement *una corda* ("one string")—that is, using one of the pedals to shift the entire keyboard action so that the hammers strike only a single string. Orchestra and soloist alternately present their respective ideas. Neither gives ground at first, but the tutti eventually diminishes in volume. At m. 47, the soloist moves on to a new idea, a soaring melody that sounds very much like a singer's aria. This gives way to a dramatic series of simultaneous runs and trills in an extended (and written out) cadenza. Beethoven asks the soloist to increase the sound first to two strings, then to the full complement of three, before receding back to the original *una corda* sound. (On a modern piano, this effect can only be simulated by a careful use of the *una corda* pedal and the full (*tre corde*) pedal; the *due corde* effect is no longer available per se.)

At least some listeners have interpreted this movement as a musical reenactment of part of the myth of Orpheus and Euridice. According to this interpretation, m. 1–5 and 14–18 represent Orpheus descending into the underworld and confronting Charon; m. 38–48 represent him charming Charon with music; m. 47–54 represent him crossing the river Styx to the underworld to retrieve Euridice; m. 55–63 (the solo cadenza) represent his doubts about whether Euridice is still behind him as he ascends back to the world of the living; and finally, the empty-sounding final cadence reflects his despair at the second loss of his beloved. Although Beethoven himself left no direct evidence to support this interpretation, accounts by friends and acquaintances suggest that it is at least plausible.

121 Piano Sonata in C Major, Op. 53
("Waldstein"), first movement (1804)

Beethoven

CD9, Track 7

Book p. 414

0:56.5

4:55.4

5:33.34

6:44.73

7:54.53

No. 121 Beethoven: Piano Sonata in C Major, Op. 53   ■   **203**

CD10, Track 2
Book p. 414

The gulf between music written for amateurs and professionals expanded greatly during the 19th century. Beethoven's piano sonatas, although widely admired, were repeatedly criticized during his lifetime for their technical difficulty. His Sonata in C Major, Op. 53, completed in 1804 and dedicated to Count Waldstein, an early patron from Bonn, may seem relatively undemanding compared to later works, but its rapid passagework and broken octave scales put it beyond the reach of most amateurs at the time it was written.

In a break with what had become standard practice in the Classical era, the exposition of the first movement modulates to the mediant (E major, which later becomes E minor) instead of the dominant (G major). This kind of modulation reflects the increasing chromaticism of 19th-century harmonic practice and the consequent erosion of the polarity between tonic and dominant that had characterized the formal structures of the mid- to late 18th century. Later composers working within the conventions of sonata form would often modulate to keys other than the dominant or relative major.

While looking forward in terms of its technical demands and harmonic structure, the "Waldstein" also looks back for thematic inspiration, illustrating Beethoven's ability to transform a predecessor's idea into an entirely new creation. The opening bears striking parallels to Haydn's String Quartet Op. 33, No. 3 (Anthology 2/105, discussed in Chapter 12). Like Haydn's quartet, Beethoven's sonata is in the key of C major, begins with a series of repeated notes, introduces its thematic idea in fragments, and repeats this idea on a series of unusual scale degrees before finally reestablishing the tonic (m. 14). We do not know if Beethoven was conscious of these underlying connections, but we do know that he studied the works of Haydn and Mozart carefully, even copying out entire quartets or quartet movements on occasion to better understand their craft of composition.

First movement

1:14

1:47

2:35.86

4:23

5:55.74

6:43.62

No. 122 Beethoven: String Quartet in B♭ Major, Op. 130   ■   **209**

8:54.89

0:22.87

Like his piano sonatas, Beethoven's string quartets also reflect the trend toward increasing technical difficulty. Good amateurs could readily have performed the six quartets he published as Op. 18 in 1801, but not the three substantially longer quartets he published as Op. 59 in 1808. Beethoven's late quartets—Opuses 127, 130, 132, and 135, composed between 1824 and 1826—are among the most challenging works he wrote in any genre, for performers and listeners alike. Contemporary listeners had never heard anything quite like the opening of the Quartet in B♭ Major, Op. 130. The music is full of unexpected starts and stops. What appears at first to be a slow introduction, for example, turns out to be an integral part of the sonata-form exposition. And instead of modulating to the expected dominant (F) in the exposition, Beethoven dramatically overshoots it (m. 51) and lands instead in the unlikely key of G♭ (♭VI, m. 55).

Subsequent movements are similarly full of formal and technical surprises. The second movement scherzo, marked *Presto,* runs less than two minutes in many performances, even those that observe all of Beethoven's repeat signs. (The first movement, in contrast usually runs between 12 and 13 minutes.) The third movement, marked *Andante con moto, ma non troppo,* is a study in equal-voiced texture. In the opening measures, for example, melody and accompaniment are nearly indistinguishable. The fourth movement, a German dance (*Alla danza tedesca*) also features unusual textures, especially toward the end (m. 129–140). Here the melodic line bounces from instrument to instrument, each playing solo but completing together a continuous line of melody. Some later writers have compared this technique to pointillism, a painting technique developed in the late 19th century in which recognizable images are created from a pattern of tiny, discrete dots of color.

The fifth movement of this quartet, labeled "Cavatina," is of particular interest. In Italian opera, *cavatina* designated any introductory aria sung by a main character. In Germany, however, the term was reserved largely for simple arias of an introspective quality, free of virtuosic display, and it is clearly this kind of cavatina that Beethoven had in mind. It is in effect an aria without words, with the first violin clearly imitating a solo voice. Many composers had written aria-like string quartet movements before; what makes this one different is the interplay of the ensemble as a whole. The other three voices create a texture that is at once homophonic and contrapuntal. The soloist, moreover, "sings" in a voice that is almost sobbing, choking—as Beethoven marks it, *beklemmt* ("as if caught in a vise"). Violinists produce this effect by reducing pressure on the bow, letting it ride lightly across the string. The resulting tone is neither full nor beautiful, but nonetheless dramatically moving.

The original finale of Op. 130 was an enormous fugue that Beethoven later published as a separate work with its own opus number, the *Grosse Fuge* ("Great Fugue"), Op. 133. This work has justly been called Beethoven's equivalent to *The Art of Fugue,* Johann Sebastian Bach's compilation of fugues on a single theme. It is no coincidence that it should have originally been intended to provide the capstone to a work so thoroughly occupied with issues of texture. In its place, Beethoven wrote a shorter finale in which an apparently simple opening, based on a kind of folk-like dance, becomes increasingly complex, with a remarkable multiplicity of textures.

4:14

5:07

123 Three Lieder
Franz Schubert (1797–1828)

123a Erlkönig, D. 328 (1815)

CD10, Track 5
Book p. 416

0:50.22

1:28.06

1:51.97

2:12.86

2:30.95   2:55.3   3:25.0

Wer reitet so spät durch Nacht und Wind?	Who rides so late through night and wind?
Es ist der Vater mit seinem Kind;	It is the father with his child;
er hat den Knaben wohl in dem Arm,	He holds the boy fast in his arms
er fasst ihn sicher, er hält ihn warm.	He holds him tightly, he holds him warm.
Mein Sohn, was birgst du so bang dein Gesicht?	My son, why do you hide your face so anxiously?
Siehst, Vater, du den Erlkönig nicht?	Do you not see, father, the elf-king?
den Erlkönig mit Kron und Schweif?	The elf-king with crown and train?
Mein Sohn, es ist ein Nebelstreif.	My son, it is a streak of clouds.
"Du liebes Kind, komm, geh mit mir!	"You dear child, come with me!
gar schöne Spiele spiel' ich mit dir;	Such wonderful games I will play with you;
manch bunte Blumen sind an dem Strand,	So many beautiful flowers are on the shore,
meine Mutter hat manch gülden Gewand."	My mother has many a golden robe."
Mein Vater, mein Vater, und hörest du nicht,	My father, my father, do you not yet hear,
was Erlenkönig mir leise verspricht?	What the elf-king softly promises me?
Sei ruhig, bleibe ruhig, mein Kind:	Be calm, stay calm, my child:
in dürren Blättern säuselt der Wind.	Through the dry leaves rustles the wind.
"Willst, feiner Knabe, du mit mir gehen?	"Will you, dear child, come with me?
meine Töchter sollen dich warten schön;	My daughters shall wait on you well;
meine Töchter führen den nächtlichen Reihn	my daughters dance at night
und wiegen und tanzen und singen dich ein."	and will cradle and dance and sing to you."
Mein Vater, mein Vater, und siehst du nichtdort	My father, my father, do you not see there
Erlkönigs Töchter am düstern Ort?	Elf-king's daughters in the desolate place?
Mein Sohn, mein Sohn, ich seh es genau,	My son, my son, I see it clearly,
es scheinen die alten Weiden so grau.	The old fields appear so gray.
"Ich liebe dich, mir reizt deine schöne Gestalt,	"I love you, your lovely form charms me,
und bist du nicht willig, so brauch ich Gewalt."	and if you're unwilling, I'll use force."
"Mein Vater, mein Vater, jetzt fasst er mich an!	"My father, my father, now he grabs me!
Erlkönig hat mir ein Leids getan!"	Elf-king has done me harm!"
Dem Vater grauset's, er reitet geschwind,	The father, filled with horror, rides fast,
er hält in Armen das ächzende Kind,	He holds in his arms the groaning child,
erreicht den Hof mit Müh und Not;	Reaches the courtyard with toil and trouble,
in seinen Armen das Kind war tot.	In his arms the child was dead.

123b **Prometheus,** D. 674 (1819)

CD10, Track 6

Book p. 416

2:28.22

1:14

1:52

Bedecke deinen Himmel, Zeus, mit Wolkendunst,
und übe, dem Knaben gleich, der Disteln köpft,

an Eichen dich und Bergeshöh'n;
musst mir meine Erde doch lassen steh'n,
und meine Hütte, die du nicht gebaut,
und meinen Herd, um de Gluth du mich
   beneidest.
Ich kenne nichts Ärmeres unter der Sonn',
als euch, Götter!
Ihr nährt kümmerlich
vom Opfersteuern und Gebetshauch eure
   Majestät,
und darbtet,
wären nicht Kinder und Bettler hoffnungsvolle
   Thoren.
Da ich ein Kind war, nicht wusste wo aus noch
   ein,
kehrt'ich mein verirrtes Auge zur Sonne,
als wenn d'rüber wär'ein Ohr, zu hören meine
   Klage,
ein Herz, wie mein's,
sich des Bedrängten zu erbarmen.
Wer half mir wider der Titanen Übermuth?
Wer rettete vom Tode mich, von Sclaverei?
Hast du nicht alles selbst vollendet,
heilig glühend Herz?
Und glühtest jung und gut, betrogen,
Rettungsdank dem Schlafenden da droben?

Ich dich ehren? Wofür?
Hast du die Schmerzen gelindert je des
   Beladenen?
Ich dich ehren? Wofür?
Hast du die Thränen gestillet je des
   Geängsteten?
Hat mich nicht zum Manne geschmiedet die
   allmächtige Zeit
und das ewige Schicksal, meine Herrn und
   deine?
Wähntest du etwa, ich sollte das Leben hassen,
in Wüsten fliehen,
weil nicht alle Blüthenträume reiften?
Hier sitz' ich,
forme Menschen nach meinem Bilde,
ein Geschlecht, das mir gleich sei,
zu leiden, zu weinen, zu geniessen und zu
   freuen sich,
und dein nicht zu achten, wie ich!

Cover your heaven, Zeus, with cloud-dust
and practice—like the youth who blows the tops
   off dandelions—
on oak trees and mountaintops.
You must, however, let my earth be,
and my hut, which you did not build,
and my hearth, whose glow you envy.

I know nothing more pitiful under the sun
than you gods!
You nourish yourselves miserably
on sacrifice and the breath of prayers

and would wither away,
were not children and beggars hopeful fools.

When I was a child, not knowing anything,

I turned my mistaken eye to the sun,
as if up above there were an ear to hear my cry,

a heart, like mine,
that could comfort the oppressed.
Who helped me against the arrogance of Titans?
Who saved me from death, from slavery?
Have you not perfected everything yourself,
holy, glowing heart?
And glowed young and well, deceived,
Saying thanks for rescue to the sleeping one up
   there?

I should honor you? For what?
Have you ameliorated the pain for the
   downtrodden?
I should honor you? For what?
Have you ever stilled the tears of the anguished?

Has not the almighty time forged me into a man

and the eternal fate, the masters of both you and
   me?
Did you perhaps think I should hate life,
flee to the deserts,
just because not all dreams of flowers grow ripe?
Here I sit,
formed human according to my image,
a race that resembles me,
to suffer, to weep, to enjoy and to rejoice,

and not to obey you but rather myself!

123c Wanderers Nachtlied, D. 768 (1824)

CD10, Track 7

Book p. 417

Über allen Gipfeln ist Ruh,
in allen Wipfeln spürest du kaum einen Hauch;
die Vöglein schweigen,
schweigen im Walde.
Warte nur, balde ruhest du auch.

Over all summits is calm,
in every corner you feel barely a breath;
the birds are silent,
silent in the woods.
Wait yet, soon you, too, shall rest.

From the perspective of form, songs generally fall into one of three categories: strophic, modified strophic, or through-composed. In strophic form, the simplest of the three, each verse (strophe) of a poem is set to the same music. In modified strophic form, as in a variation on a theme, the music varies from strophe to strophe—with melodic embellishment, for example, or alteration of texture or harmony—but remains otherwise recognizably the same. A through-composed song, in contrast, has no recognizable pattern of repetition, and often no repetition at all. *Erlkönig* is in modified strophic form; *Prometheus* and *Wanderers Nachtlied* are through-composed; for an example of a strophic song, see Reichardt's setting of Goethe's *Kennst du das Land* (Anthology 2/114).

Song composers in the 19th century were judged according to the extent to which their music enhanced the words of the poems they set. The repetitive rhythmic insistence of Franz Schubert's *Erlkönig* ("Elf-king") reflects the content and iambic meter of Goethe's strophic poem. Schubert, however, goes beyond this rhythmic device to magnify the poem's emotional force in his modified-strophic setting. *Erlkönig* tells a chilling tale of a father riding home with his feverish son in his arms. The boy hears the Elf-king calling to him with seductive blandishments and cries out in fear as his father tries vainly to calm him. When they arrive, the boy is dead in his father's arms. The poem has four voices—a narrator, the Elf-king, the boy, and the father—and Schubert gives each of them a distinctive character through the strategic use of key, mode, texture, and register.

Free verse, as is found in a poem like Goethe's *Prometheus,* calls for a flexible musical structure. Schubert's through-composed setting emphasizes the declamatory tone and irregular rhythms of the poetry. The music and the text are equally dramatic. In Greek myth it was Prometheus who, against the will of Zeus, gave fire to humanity. As punishment for this transgression, Prometheus was chained to a rock, where every day an eagle came to eat out his liver, which grew back every night. In the poem the unrepentant Prometheus hurls scorn and defiance on Zeus. Schubert's setting conveys this defiance with the dotted rhythms of the piano introduction. The passages marked "Recit." (for recitative) are to be sung in the relatively free, declamatory style characteristic of operatic recitative.

Goethe's *Wanderers Nachtlied* ("Wanderer's Night Song"), a brief poem of a single strophe, elicited from Schubert an intense attention to detail. The limited melodic motion and straightforward rhythms of the opening capture the sense of calm that pervades the text ("Over all summits is calm…") and make the subsequent syncopation (m. 5–8) all the more pronounced. The repeated horn call-like figures in m. 9–13 take on added importance through repetition. In so brief a setting, every gesture carries added weight. Even the one-measure epilogue in the piano (m. 14) resonates with significance, given the remarkably small scale of this work.

124 Three Settings of Goethe's **Kennst du das Land**

For translations of this text, see No. II/114.

CD10, Track 8

Book p. 417

124a Kennst du das Land (Mignons Gesang), D. 321 (1815)

Schubert

0:49.23

222 ■ No. 124a Schubert: *Kennst du das Land*

3:45.59

1:25.4

1:41.78

10

Langsam und sehr ausdrucksvoll

Kennst du das Land, wo die Zi - tro - nen blühn,

im dunklen Laub die Gold - o - rangen glühn,

ein sanfter Wind vom blau - en Him - mel weht,

die Myr - te still und hoch der Lor - beer steht,

225

1:17.37　　　　　　　　　　　　　　　　　　1:47.3　　2:18.25

4:19.0

Different composers were often drawn to the same text, bringing to it a variety of interpretations that reflect changing styles and expanding musical options. For example, Johann Friedrich Reichardt's late-18th-century setting of Goethe's poemKennst du das Land?" ("Do You Know the Land?") under the title "Italien" (Anthology 2/114), is relatively straightforward, with a limited melodic range and folklike diatonicism. Later settings—like those by Schubert, Schumann, and Hugo Wolf—have more intricate vocal lines, richer textures, and increasingly chromatic harmonies that reflect the 19th-century's ever-expanding harmonic vocabulary. Wolf's setting, in particular, illustrates the move away from the aesthetic of simplicity among composers of the latter part of the 19th-century. HisMignon" focuses on the second part of each strophe ("Kennst du es [ihn] wohl? Dahin!"), initiated by the accompaniment (marked *Belebt,* in measures 21, 58, and 99), to provide structural background through repetition and melodic climax. The first half of each strophe is more freely composed, with multiple changes of tempo, key, and dynamic level, building in intensity until the final strophe, in which Mignon pleads with Wilhelm, "Dahin! Dahin geht unser Weg! o Vater, lass uns ziehn!" (The version included on the CD set is Wolf's second of two orchestrations [1893] of "Mignon.")

125 Beautiful Dreamer (1862)
Stephen Foster (1826–1864)

CD10, Track 11
Book p. 420

queen of my song,.... List while I woo thee with soft me - lo - dy;......
beam on my heart,.... E'en as the morn on the streamlet and sea;......

Gone are the cares of life's bu-sy throng, Beau-ti - ful dreamer, a-wake un - to
Then will all clouds of sor-row de - part, Beau-ti - ful dreamer, a-wake un - to

me!.......... Beau -ti - ful dreamer, a - wake un - to me!...........
me!.......... Beau -ti - ful dreamer, a - wake un - to me!...........

ad lib.   *a tempo.*

Published by permission of WM. A. POND & Co., owners of the copyright.

Beautiful Dreamer epitomizes the 19th-century American parlor song, so called because of its place of performance in the equivalent of today's living room—which is to say, at home, in a domestic setting. Its tone is sentimental and earnest, its strophic form straightforward, its technical demands extremely modest.

A note on the edition: The edition here reproduces a typical late-19th-century edition of the song. It is not particularly attractive but the movable type used here—note the many visible breaks between the individual pieces of type, particularly in the staff lines—made this kind of publication inexpensive to produce and thus affordable to a larger base of consumers. Metal type could withstand far more pressure over a longer period of time than the more malleable (and more attractive but less durable) metal alloy plates commonly used for engraving.

126 **V chetyrjokh stenakh** ("In Four Walls"),
from the song cycle **Bez solnca** ("Sunless")
(1874)

Modeste Mussorgsky (1839–1881)

CD10, Track 12
Book p. 421

Komnatka tesnaja, tikhaja, milaja,
Ten' neprogljadnaja, ten' bezotvetnaja,
Duma glubokaja, pesnja unylaja,

V b'jushchemsja serdce nadezhda zavetnaja.

Bystryj polet za mgnoven'jem mgnovenija,
Vzor nepodvizhnyj na schast'je dalekoje,
Mnogo somnenija, mnogo terpenija,
Vot ona, noch' moja, noch' odinokaja.

I lie here in my room, sleeplessly,
Dark fathomless night all around me.
Gently a sigh is heard, one sad complaining word.
A faint hope remains in my aching heart.

Every moment rushes by so quickly,
Anxiously gazing on joy that is far away,
Ever doubting, ever suffering—
So the lonely night passes.

Mussorgsky's *V chetyrjokh stenakh* illustrates the ever-expanding presence of chromaticism in music from the later decades of the 19th century, as well as Mussorgsky's penchant for a naturalistic kind of declamation that fits well with his often dark and brooding texts. (Native or well-trained speakers of Russian can add an extra bite to the text with clear pronunciation of its frequently complex consonants and consonant combinations.) The recitative-like declamation elicits a chordal piano part, sprinkled with brief parallel countermelodies.

127 Trio in D minor, op. 11:
third movement (Lied)
Fanny Mendelssohn Hensel (1805–1847)

CD10, Track 13

Book p. 423

1:02.56

128 Mazurka in A minor, Op. 17, No. 4 (1833)

Frédéric Chopin (1810–1849)

CD10, Track 14

Book p. 423

1:38

Fanny Mendelssohn Hensel (her married name from 1829) composed numerous character piano pieces, including sets of *Lieder ohne WorteLied,* but the composer skillfully alters it each time it returns: changing the notes (and harmonies) slightly, allowing each instrument to have a turn at it, or changing the nature of the accompaniment. This creates a satisfying, almost Classical sense of both variety and unity. The 19th-century element is the intimacy of music written for salon rather than concert hall use, to be shared among participants and a small audience in tune with the domestic spirit of the era.

2:01.36

Chopin's Mazurka Op. 17, No. 4, is one of many 19th-century character pieces modeled on a particular dance—in this case, the mazurka, a Polish peasant dance in triple meter, often with an accent on the second or third beat. The work is harmonically ambiguous in several ways. It opens with three three-note chords that do not follow a harmonic progression in any conventional sense. The focus, instead, appears to be the motion of the middle note in each chord, the only one of the three to change. The progression B-C-D within the framework of the F and A in the outer voices prefigures a harmony that will prove repeatedly elusive. The cadence at the end of m. 4 can be read as an F major chord in first inversion (A-C-F), but the absence of B♭ gives the work more a modal sound, either Lydian (a scale on F without the B♭) or Aeolian (a scale on A with no accidentals). The chromatic descent of linked thirds beginning in m. 9 (F♯-D♯ followed by F♮-D♮) further undermines the sense of a strong tonal center. Chopin creates the expectation of a strong cadence on A minor at the downbeat to m. 13, but delays it until m. 20. And even then, he gives us just enough stability in A minor to make us think we know where we are going, and that the piece has a tonal center. The middle section of this work, by contrast (m. 61–92) hammers away at A major triads so relentlessly that it seems to take all the energy it can muster to move to a dominant harmony even briefly. But with the return of the opening section at m. 93, we are thrust back into the realm of harmonic ambiguity. At the end of the piece, Chopin repeats the opening sequence of harmonically ambiguous chords followed by an A-C-F triad, giving us a conclusion but no harmonic closure.

A harmonically ambiguous opening had many distinguished precedents. One need think only of such works as Mozart's "Dissonant" Quartet, K. 465, or Haydn's "Drumroll" Symphony, No. 103 (Anthology No. 106). But a harmonically ambiguous close like this one was a phenomenon essentially new to the 19th century.

Performance notes: The great pianist Artur Rubinstein (1887–1982) recorded the complete Mazurkas of Chopin at three different points in his career (in 1938–1939, 1952–1953, 1965–1966), and all have found a ready audience among the pianist's admirers, for each reflects a different stage of the artist's long career. The recording here is from the 1960s.

2:58.5

CD11, Track 1
Book p. 425

Prelude in C Major

Prelude in A Minor

Prelude in G Major

Prelude in E Minor

Chopin's *Preludes,* Op. 28, consist of 24 individual works presented in an order that follow the circle of fifths, moving systematically through all 24 major and minor keys of the twelve-note scale (from C major and A minor to G major and E minor, and so forth). The homage to J. S. Bach's *Well-Tempered Clavier* is unmistakable (Anthology 1/95). The first Prelude, in C major, imitates the broken chordal writing in the corresponding prelude of the first book of Bach's collection and uses harmonic progressions rather than a distinctive melodic line to create a sense of overall shape. And even though Chopin's preludes lack fugues, many of them explore unusual possibilities of voice leading. In the A minor Prelude, for example, a back-and-forth half-step motion in one voice is framed by another voice making leaps of a tenth. The Prelude in G Major is rather like an etude, emphasizing a single constant motion throughout in the rapid passagework in the left hand. And the Prelude in E minor recreates the mood of a lament, possibly from a tragic heroine in an opera; the steady chromatic descent in the lower voices echo the age-old connection of the falling chromatic line with suffering and pain.

CD11, Track 5
Book p. 428

*) The Princess M. Czartorvska, Frau F. Streicher, and Dr F. von Hiller maintain the authenticity of this Eb in opposition to the D of earlier editions.

2:52.14

4:14.69

Although composers in the generations after Beethoven never abandoned the multimovement sonata entirely, it gradually gave way to larger-scale forms in a single movement such as the ballade, cultivated by Chopin, Liszt, Brahms, and Fauré, and the scherzo, cultivated by Chopin and Brahms. Chopin's Ballade in G minor, Op. 23, is an extended work with many elements of sonata form. After a brief introduction (m. 1–7), Chopin establishes two main key areas, G minor (m. 8–44) and E♭ major (m. 67–93), connected by a transition section (m. 44–67). Although the modulation here is from i to VI rather than the more typical i to III, the form of this opening corresponds to the conventions of a sonata-form exposition. Then, as in the development section of a sonata-form movement, Chopin takes the two main ideas through a variety of new key areas and manipulates them thematically before introducing a new idea (m. 138). The recapitulation deviates from the conventions of sonata form in that the theme originally presented in E♭ major returns in that same key (m. 166) rather than in the tonic. Only later does the first theme finally return to reestablish the tonic (m. 194). A coda (m. 208–264) introduces yet another new theme. Given so many deviations from the conventions of sonata form, it would be misleading to say that Chopin's G minor Ballade is "in sonata form." At the same time, it would be wrong to deny altogether that it reflects the influence of sonata form. Many 19th-century instrumental works share this kind of formal ambiguity, simultaneously operating within and pushing beyond the conventions of established forms.

It was long believed that Chopin based each of his four Ballades on one of the poetic ballads of the 19th-century Polish poet Adam Mickiewicz, but no evidence supports this belief. The G minor Ballade nevertheless projects a strong sense of narrative direction. The powerful unison opening is a call to attention, and the rhythmic regularity of the subsequent moderato (m. 8–32) conveys a sense of metered verse. Each section of the work embodies a particular affect, moving from the resigned (m. 8–32) to lyrical (m. 68–93), ecstatic (m. 106–124) to agitated (m. 124–137), waltz-like (m. 138–154) to furious (m. 208–242). The catastrophic conclusion (m. 244–end), with its abrupt ending, brings to mind the abrupt and tragic end of Goethe's well-known poetic ballad *Erlkönig* (see Anthology No. 121a for Schubert's setting).

131 Galop de bal (ca. 1840)
Franz Liszt (1811–1886)

CD11, Track 6
Book p. 428

The galop was a fashionable group dance of the mid-19th century that moved at a lively pace, with steady accents on both the first and third beat of every duple measure. In keeping with the genre's origins in dance, Liszt constructs this "Galop of the Ball" around units of 4, 8, and 16 measures. But the unprepared harmonic deflection to ♭VI in m. 17 adds a nice twist against the rhythmic regularity, as does the chromatic instability over a pedal point tonic toward the end.

132 Carnaval, Op. 9 (excerpts) (1835)
Robert Schumann

CD11, Track 7

Book p. 428

248 ■ No. 132 Schumann: *Carnaval*

Schumann's *Carnaval,* Op. 9 (1835), is a cycle of character pieces ranging from the simple to the complex, linked by the common theme of Carnival, the brief season of revelry immediately preceding the penitential season of Lent. During Carnival—whose only high-profile manifestation in the United States today is the Mardi Gras celebration in New Orleans—conventional social standards are set aside. In Schumann's time it was perfectly acceptable for people to go about in costume and do behind masks what they could only dream of doing openly.

Like the season for which it is named, many of the movements of Schumann's *Carnaval* contain elements of intrigue, impersonation, excess, and downright nonsense. Musically, the entire cycle is based on a riddle, the key to which is given in the movement entitled "Sphinxes." In Greek mythology, the sphinx was a creature who posed a riddle to passersby, killing those who couldn't solve it. Here, Schumann presents a series of brief motivic ideas in archaic breves. The key to the riddle is to be found in the German names for the notes of each motivic idea. Adding "s" to any note name in German designates it as flat. Thus Eb is "Es" and Ab is "As." In addition, Germans designate Bᅢ with the letter "H." With this in mind, we can see that one of the sequences (Eb-C-B-A) spells "Schumann" in an abbreviated form (Es=S,C,H,A) and the other two (Ab-C-B and A-Eb-C-B) spell "Asch" (As,C,H and A,S,C,H).

"Asch" is the hometown of Ernestine von Fricken, who was Schumann's fiancée when he wrote *Carnaval.* Schumann embeds the second and third sequences of notes throughout the individual pieces in *Carnaval.* The opening notes in the upper part of "Papillons," for example, are A, Eb, C, and Cb (= Bᅢ = H). The opening of "Chiarina" is Ab, C, Bᅢ (=H).

As the Sphinxes suggest, *Carnaval* is an autobiographical work: Schumann uses the mask of music to say things he would not otherwise have ventured to acknowledge openly. Consider, for example, the trio of movements labeled "Chiarina," "Chopin," and "Estrella." Chiarina was the nickname of the fifteen-year-old Clara Wieck, the daughter of his own former piano teacher. Schumann would later marry Clara, but when he wrote *Carnaval* he was engaged to Ernestine, whose nickname was Estrella. In a gesture clearly anticipating the inevitable end of his engagement to Ernestine, Schumann marks "Estrella" to be played *con affetto* ("with affection") and, in pointed contrast, marks "Chiarina" to be played *passionate* ("passionately"). The two women in question surely grasped the significance of these indications. The two movements are mediated by one named after Chopin, a composer Schumann greatly admired, who had paid personal visits to both Clara and Robert in September 1835. In an imitation of Chopin's style, the piece titled "Chopin" has a graceful and soaring melodic line, an elaborately arpeggiated accompaniment, and a clear homophonic texture. It also offers plenty of opportunity for *tempo rubato* in performance.

CD11, Track 12
Book p. 433

1:07

Like the song, the character piece became increasingly chromatic in the latter part of the 19th century. Liszt's *Nuages gris* ("Gray Clouds"), written in 1881 but unpublished at the composer's death two years later, opens with a rising fourth, followed by a rising augmented fourth and a descending G minor triad in m. 2. In its context, this triad sounds neither particularly triadic nor like a triad in the tonic (which is in fact what it is). Throughout this brief piece, Liszt alludes to the tonic through the leading tone of F♯ without actually presenting any strong statement of G minor. Even the final chord juxtaposes a G-B♮ dyad with an open A-E fifth in the lower voices. The music seems to float like the clouds evoked in its title, with little sense of any forward motion. In this respect, it anticipates the Impressionist style of the late 19th and early 20th centuries (see Textbook, Chapter 20).

134 Caprices, Op. 1, No. 24, in A minor
(ca. 1810)

Niccolò Paganini (1782–1840)

CD11, Track 13
Book p. 433

Paganini's *Caprices,* Op. 1 (published in 1820 but probably written at least a decade before), are 24 in number and pay homage to a set of 24 caprices published by Pietro Locatelli, an earlier violin virtuoso, in 1733. The last of Paganini's 24 caprices makes an unusually wide variety of techical demands on the violinist. Formally, it is a set of variations on a theme, with each variation highlighting a particular technique:

- Variation 1: Spiccato arpeggiation. This technique involves bouncing the bow lightly on the string.
- Variation 2: Bariolage. The rapid and repeated alternation between two adjacent strings, one open, the other fingered.
- Variation 3: Octaves. Because the violin does not feature fixed pitches, like a piano, octaves require absolutely perfect placement of two fingers in relation to each other.
- Variation 4: High chromatic passages. The higher the hand moves on the fingerboard, the smaller the physical space between the finger placements of the individual notes.
- Variation 5: String crossing. This variation requires the player to move quite rapidly between strings.
- Variation 6: Thirds and octaves. Again, both pitches must be perfectly fingered.
- Variation 7: Bowing. The player must pick up and replace the bow in a downstroke rapidly in succession while playing a triplet figure that moves through all registers of the instrument.
- Variation 8: Triple stopping. The performer rolls a series of chords on three different notes, each played on a different string.
- Variation 9: Left-hand pizzicato. The player must alternate rapidly between notes played with the bow and notes plucked with the left hand (not the right hand, as in normal pizzicato).
- Variation 10: High position. The performer must execute rapid runs in a very high register.
- Variation 11: Successive double stops.
- Finale: Long runs and successive double stops.

4:12

135 **Etudes d'exécution transcendante,**
No. 1 in C Major (1838; revised 1851)
Franz Liszt (1811–1886)

CD11, Track 14
Book p. 437

Liszt's *Etudes d'exécution transcendante,* as their title suggests, require a technical facility that transcends the ordinary. The first of these etudes, in C major, clearly fits into the tradition of C major works that open large, systematically ordered sets: Bach's C Major Prelude in the *Well-Tempered Clavier* (Anthology 1/95), Chopin's C Major Prelude in his *Preludes,* Op. 24 (Anthology No. 128), as well as the opening C Major Etude in Chopin's *Etudes* for piano, Op. 10. (Liszt follows the same pattern in these etudes that Chopin had used in his preludes: a circle of descending fifths in the major keys, with each major-mode work followed by one in the relative minor.) But from the perspective of technical demands, Liszt's opening salvo in these "Transcendental" etudes leaves all earlier works in its wake. Robert Schumann, reviewing an earlier version of these etudes, called them "studies in storm and dread . . . fit for ten or twelve players in the world."

136 The Banjo (1855)
Louis Moreau Gottschalk (1829–1869)

CD11, Track 15

Book p. 437

0:09.82

0:53.81

No. 136 Gottschalk: *The Banjo* ■ **255**

1:21.45

1:59.54

2:46.05

Gottschalk's *The Banjo* captures on the piano the idiomatic vitality of the banjo, that quintessentially American instrument. The music's constant strumming rhythms and jaunty syncopations anticipate the ragtime style that would become popular in the United States a few decades later (see Textbook, Chapter 24). Subtitled "An American Sketch," the work incorporates a clever reference to Stephen Foster's immensely popular song *The Camptown Races,* the theme of which begins to creep in around m. 178, blossoms shortly thereafter, and then is swallowed up in the volley of rapid-fire "strumming" that ends the work. In a concession to public sales, Gottschalk at various points offers alternative, slightly easier ways of performing some of the work's more difficult passages; these are marked "Facilité" in the score and notated above the standard line of music.

137a Act I, Scene 2, cavatina (Figaro):
"Largo al factotum"

CD12, Track 1
Book p. 440

Note: This edition is a piano-vocal reduction of Rossini's original score for voices and orchestra.

0:36.84

1:29.1

1:48.59

2:59.31

3:43.2

137b Act I, Scene 5, cavatina (Rosina): "Una voce poco fa"

A room in the house of Dr. Bartolo. The windows closed with Venetian blinds. Rosina has a letter in her hand.

U - na   vo - ce po-co   fa   qui nel cor   mi ri - suo - nò,   il mio
There's a   voice that I en-shrine   In my heart,   and none must know;   Ah, Lin-

0:37

1:29.16

2:23.37

No. 137 Rossini: *Il Barbiere di Siviglia* ■ 267

3:18.02

Rossini's *Il Barbiere di Siviglia* ("The Barber of Seville") narrates a series of intrigues that entangle a nobleman (Count Almaviva) who, disguised as the poor student "Lindoro," seeks to win the affections of a beautiful young woman (Rosina), who stands under the watchful eye of her guardian, the prim and proper Doctor Bartolo. The town's barber, Figaro, acts as a go-between for the many complications of the plot.

Figaro's opening number, *Largo al factotum* ("Make way for the factotum"), does a marvelous job introducing the title character. He half complains, half boasts that his services are in such demand among people of quality that he is always busy. Constantly repeating the same lines of text, Figaro works himself into frenzy, imitating people calling him—"Figaro! Figaro!"—in that famous three note melody (m. 187–192) that has come to be indelibly associated with his character. "One at a time!" he half shouts to himself in response.

Rosina's *Una voce poco fa* ("A voice a short while ago") is very much in the *bel canto* tradition and draws an equally sharp characterization. Like many arias of this period, it consists of two sections, a slow opening and a lively conclusion, known as the *cabaletta*. Rosina sings while writing a letter to Lindoro—who is in fact Count Almaviva in disguise. After declaring Lindoro her chosen suitor, she professes to be "docile, respectful, and obedient." The music, however, gives the lie to this claim, changing from reserved to lively and spontaneous in the cabaletta, as she goes on to sing: "But if you push me the wrong way, I'll be a viper, and the last laugh will be on you." By the time she returns to her profession of docility, the feistiness of the music has infected the orchestra, leaving no doubt that the music, not the words, represents Rosina's true character.

The performance. Note the considerable liberties the singers take with the written notation, particularly in Rosina's aria (for example, at m. 32–42 and 89–98). This is part of the *bel canto* tradition, in which singers were expected to embellish their parts, often quite elaborately. At times, the music calls out for embellishment, as at the cadenza-like high G♯ with the fermata at m. 90. But even seemingly florid passages (such as m. 39–40) are fair game for alteration. This practice prevailed during Rossini's era and has continued down to the present day. Different recordings of the same aria readily demonstrate that virtually every singer uses Rossini's notation more as a point of departure than as something to be followed precisely.

138 Rigoletto (1851)
Giuseppe Verdi (1813–1901)

138a Act I (excerpts)

CD11, Track 16

Book p. 440

Note: This edition is a piano-vocal reduction of Verdi's original score for voices and orchestra.

Sala magnifica nel palazzo ducale con porte nel fondo che mettono ad altre sale,

pure splendidamente illuminate.

Folla di Cavalieri e Dame che passeggiano nelle sale del fondo.

Paggi che vanno e vengono.

Nelle sale in fondo si vedrà bal_

_lare.

2:16

BALLATA

3:49.76

4:42.54

MINUETTO E PERIGODINO NELL'INTRODUZIONE.

ATTO.I. *SCENA II.* Entrano Dame e Cavalieri. Intanto nella sala in fondo si ballerà il Minuetto.

Tempo di Minuetto.

Strumenti sul palco.

(Il Duca va ad incontrare la Contessa di Ceprano e le dice con molta galanteria)

DUCA

Par_

LA CONTESSA DI CEPRANO

_ti_te?.. Cru_de_le!.. Se_gui_re lo spo_so m'è

DUCA.

for _ za a Ce _ prano. Ma de_e lu_mi_no_so in Cor_te tal

5:31.54

6:54

7:17.86

CORO NELL' INTRODUZIONE

7:43.88

9:51.41

10:16

11:48.28

12:44.66

13:34.55

2:48.22

3:41.88

5:08

5:45.79

No. 138 Verdi: *Rigoletto* ■ **297**

7:04.95

7:59.4

12:29.8

304 ■ No. 138 Verdi: *Rigoletto*

14:33.8

QUARTETTO

0:45.0

308 ■ No. 138 Verdi: *Rigoletto*

3:14.1

100

102

NO. 1 PRELUDE

SCENE I

A Ball-room in the Ducal Palace. Ladies and Gentlemen, Pages and Servants, cross the scene. Music is heard at a distance, and now and then bursts of laughter. Enter the Duke and Borsa.

DUKE: I am quite resolved to follow to the end My new adventure with this youthful lady.
BORSA: You mean the one you meet while going to church?
DUKE: Yes, in a lonely street, and every day she receives a visit from a dubious man.
BORSA: But does she know him?
DUKE: Yes, every Sunday for the last three months.
BORSA: Know you where she resides?
DUKE: No, I think not.

(A group of Ladies and Gentlemen cross the scene.)

BORSA: Behold those charming ladies.
DUKE: Yes, but Ceprano's wife outshines them all.
BORSA: Ah! but mind her husband, Duke.

DUKE: What matters?
BORSA: It might be spread about.
DUKE: What then—no great misfortune.

Amongst the beauties here around,
Over me none have control;
None can say, "I am preferred;"
Equal love I feel for all.
Yes, all women are to me
Like the flowers of the field.
Now to this, I am inclined,
Now to that by chance I yield.
As one flies from a great peril,
So from constancy I fly;
Those who will, may faithful be,
In freedom only does love lie.
I despise a jealous husband,
And I laugh at lover's sighs—
If a beauty strikes my fancy,
I defy one hundred eyes.

SCENA I

Sala magnifica nel Palazzo Ducale. Il Duca e Borsa che vengono da una porta del fondo.

DUCA: Della mia bella incognita borghese Toccare il fin del' avventura io voglio.
BORSA: Di quelli giovin che vedete al tempio?

DUCA: Da tre lune ogni festa.

BORSA: La sua dimora?
DUCA: In un remoto calle; Misterioso un uom v' entra ogni notte.
BORSA: E sa colei chi sia L'amante suo?
DUCA: Lo ignora.
(Un gruppo di Dame e Cavalieri attraversan la sala.)
BORSA: Quante beltà!—Mirate.
DUCA: Le vince tutte di Cepran la sposa.

BORSA: Non v' oda il Conte, o Duca—
(Piano.)
DUCA: A me che importa?
BORSA: Dirlo ad altra ei potria—
DUCA: Nè sventura per me certo saria.

Questa o quella per me pari sono
A quant' altre d' intorno mi vedo,
Del mio core l'impero non cedo
Meglio ad una che ad altra beltà.
La costoro avvenenza è qual dono
Di che il fato ne infiora la vita;
S' oggi questa mi torna gradita,
Forse un' altra doman lo sarà.
La costanza tiranna del core
Detestiamo qual morbo crudele,
Sol chi vuole si serbi fedele;
Non v' ha amor, se non v' è libertà.
De' mariti il geloso furore,
Degli amanti le smanie derido,
Anco d' Argo i cent' occhi disfido
Se mi punge una qualche beltà.

SCENA II

Detti, il Conte di Ceprano, che segue da lungi la sua sposa seguita da altro Cavaliere. Dame e Signora entrano da varie parti.

DUCA: *(Alla Signora di Cep., movendo ad incontrarla con molta galanteria.)* Partite? Crudele!

CEP: Seguire le sposo
M'è forza a Ceprano.

DUCA: Ma dee luminoso
In Corte tal astro qual sole brillare.
Per voi qui ciascuno dovrà palpitare.
Per voi già possente la fiamma d' amore
Inebria, conquide, distrugge il mio core.
(Con enfasi, baciandole la mano.)

CEP: Calmatevi—

DUCA: No.
(Le da il braccio ed esce con lei.)

SCENA III

Detti e Rigoletto che s'incontra nel Signor di Ceprano; poi Cortigiani.

RIG: In testa che avete,
Signor di Ceprano?
(Ceprano fa un gesto d'impazienza e segue il Duca.)

RIG: *(Ai Cortigiana.)* Ei sbuffa, vedete

CORO: Che festa!

RIG: Oh sì—

BORSA: Il duca quì pur si diverte

RIG: Così non è sempre? Che nuove scorpete.
Il giuoco ed il vino, le feste, la danza
Battaglie, conviti, ben tutto gli sta.
Or della Contessa l'assedio egl avanza,

E intanto il marito fremendo ne va.
(Esce)

SCENA IV

Detti e Marullo premuroso

MAR: Gran nuova! gran nuova!

DUCA: Che avvenne? Parlate!

MAR: Stupir ne dovrete—

CORO: Narrate narrate

MAR: Ah! ah! Rigoletto—

CORO: Ebben?

MAR: Caso enorme!

CORO: Perduto ha la gobba? non è più difforme?

SCENE II

Enter Count Ceprano, watching at a distance the Countess, who is followed by a Gentleman. Ladies and Lords cross the scene.

DUKE: *(To the Countess, with great politeness.)* You go already, cruel one?

COUN: I must obey my husband, I am obliged to leave.

DUKE: But you must shine at Court,
As Venus amongst the stars—
Here all must sigh for you.
Already, behold here
A victim of your charms.

COUN: Ah! silence—

DUKE: No.
(The Duke kisses her hand.)

SCENE III

Enter Rigoletto, who meets Count Ceprano and Courtiers.

RIG: What troubles you, dear Count?
You seem in deepest thought.
(The Count makes a sign of impatience, and follows the Duke.)

RIG: *(To the Courtiers.)* The Count is furious! See.

CHO: A fine ball!

RIG: Indeed.

BORSA: And even the Duke enjoys the feast.

RIG: Is it not always so? What news is this?
Wine and feasting—dancing and games—
Battles and banquets—for him all's the same.
Now against the Countess he tries to lay the siege,
And cares not for the jealousy of her liege.
(Exit.)

SCENE IV

Enter Marullo, with great anxiety.

MAR: Great news! fine news!

CHO: Quick, what has happened, say?

MAR: You will all be surprised.

CHO: Speak on, speak on.

MAR: Ah, ah! Rigoletto—

CHO: Well

MAR: Strange case.

CHO: What, has he lost his hump? Is he now straight?

MAR: Più strana è la cosa! il pazzo possiede—

CORO: Infine?

MAR: Un amante—

CORO: Amante! Chi il crede?

MAR: Il gobbo in Cupido or s' è trasformato!

CORO: Quel mostro Cupido! Cupido beato!

SCENA V

Detti ed il Duca seguita da Rigoletto, indi Ceprano.

DUCA: Ah, più di Ceprano, importuno non v' è!
La cara sua sposa è un angiol per me.

(A Rig.)

RIG: Rapitela.

DUCA: E detto! ma il farlo?

RIG: Stassera.

DUCA: Non pensi tu al Conte?

RIG: Non c' è la prigione?

DUCA: Ah, no.

RIG: Ebben—s' esilia.

DUCA: Nemmeno, buffone.

RIG: Allora la testa—
(Indicando di farla tagliare.)

CEP: (Oh l'anima nera!)
(Da se.)

DUCA: Che di' questa testa?—
(Battendo colla mano una spalla al Conte.)

RIG: Che far di tal testa?—A cosa ella vale?

CEP: Marrano!
(Infuriato battendo la spada.)

DUCA: Fermate—
(A Cep.)

RIG: Da rider mi fa.

CORO: In furia è montato!
(Tra loro.)

DUCA: Buffone, vien quà.
(A Rig.)
A sempre tu spingi lo scherzo all' estremo.
Quell' ira che sfidi colpir ti potrà.

RIG: Che coglier mi puote? Di lor non temo;
Del duca un protetto nessun toccherà.

CEP: Vendetta dal pazzo—
(Ai Cortigiani, a parte.)

CORO: Contr' esso un rancore
Pei tristi suoi modi, di noi chi non ha?

MAR: More strange still, the foolish man possesses—

CHO: What? say—

MAR: A lover.

CHO: A lover! who could ever have thought of this?

MAR: The hump-back is transformed into a Cupid.

CHO: Oh, what a monstrous Cupid! charming Cupid!

SCENE V

Enter the Duke, followed by Rigoletto, afterwards Ceprano.

DUKE: No man can be more vexing than Ceprano.
His wife is a sweet angel.
(To Rig.)

RIG: Steal her away.

DUKE: 'Tis easier said than done.

RIG: This evening.

DUKE: You think not of the Count.

RIG: Have you no prisons?

DUKE: Ah! no.

RIG: Well, banish him.

DUKE: No, no, buffoon.

RIG: His head, then.
(Marking signs of having it cut off.)

CEP: (Villain!)
(Aside.)

DUKE: What do you mean? this head?—
(Tapping the Count on the shoulder.)

RIG: Yes, what is it good for?
What can he do with it?

CEP: Miscreant!
(Unsheathing his sword.)

DUKE: Stop—stop.
(To the count.)

RIG: He makes me laugh.

CHO: He is frantic!
(Among themselves.)

DUKE: Now, buffoon, come here.
(To Rig.)
You carry your jokes too far,
His sword might reach your heart.

RIG: I fear him not. No one will dare to teach
The favorite of the Duke.

CEP: He must be punished.
(Aside to the Courtiers.)

CHO: And who has not some injuries
To avenge on him.

CEP: Vendetta!

CORO: Ma come?

CEP: Domani, chi ha core
Sia in armi da me.

TUTTI: Sì.

CEP: A notte.

TUTTI: Sarà.

(La folla de' danzatori invades la sala.)

Tutto è gioia, tutto è festa,
Tutto invitaci a goder!
Oh, guardate, non par questa
Or la reggia del piacer!

NO. 5 ATTO
SCENA VI
Detti ed il Conte di Monterone.

MON: Ch' io gli parli. *(Dall' interno.)*

DUCA: No.

MON: Il voglio.
(Entrando.)

TUTTI: Monterone!

MON: *(fissando il Duca con nobile orgoglio.)* Sì,
Monteron—la voce mia qual tuono
Vi scuoterà dovunque—

RIG: *(al Duca, contraffacendo la voce di Mon.)*
Ch' io gli parli.
(Si avanza con ridicola gravità.)
Voi congiuraste contro noi, signore,
E noi, clementi in vero, perdonammo—
Qual vi piglia or delirio—a tutte l' ore
Di vostra figlia reclamar l' onore?

MON: *(guardando Rig. con ira sprezzante.)*
Novello insulto!—Ah sì, a turbare *(al Duca.)*
Sarò vostr' orgie—verrò a gridare,
Fino a che vegga restarsi inulto
Di mia famiglia l' atroce insulto;
E se al carnefice pur mi darete
Spettro terribile mi rivedrete,
Portante in mano il teschio mio,
Vendetta chiedere al mondo e Dio.

DUCA: Non più, arrestatelo.

RIG: È matto!

CORO: Quai detti!

MON: Oh siate entrambi voi maledetti.
(Al Duca e Rig.)
Slanciare il cane al leon morente
È vile, o duca—e tu serpente, *(a Rig.)*
Tu che d' un padre ridi al dolore,
Sii maledetto!

RIG: Che sento? orrore!
(Da se colpito.)

NO. 4 ACT 1 continued

CEP: Revenge, revenge!

CHO: But how?

CEP: If you fear not, tomorrow
Come with your swords to me.

ALL: We will.

CEP: At night.

ALL: Decreed.

(A crowd of dancers invades the scene.)

To dance, to feast, to pleasure,
Here everything invite,
Look around, does this not seem
The palace of delight.

NO. 5 ACT I
SCENE VI
Enter Count Monterone.

MON: *(from without)* I must see him.

DUKE: No, no.

MON: I will. *(Entering.)*

ALL: Monterone!

MON: *(looking at the Duke, with pride.)* Yes,
Monterone.—My voice
For ever I will raise against your crimes.

RIG: *(to the Duke, counterfeiting Mon.'s voice.)* I
must see him.
(He advances with ridiculous seriousness.)
You have conspired against our name, my lord.
And we have granted pardon—
What madness now is yours? In this glad hour
To come and claim the honor of your daughter!

MON: *(looking at Rig. with contempt.)*
A new insult! but your nefarious orgies
I will disturb. Here I will raise my voice
Until the honor of an injured family
Shall be restored.
And even if you were
To sign my death and send me to the block,
My shade will claim revenge!

DUKE: No more—arrest him.

RIG: He is mad!

CHO: He is mad!

MON: Be both for ever accursed.
(To Rig. and the Duke.)
To strike the dying lion,
'Tis base—but you, reptile,
Who dares to laugh at an old father's grief
Malediction fall on you!

RIG: What do I hear!
Oh, terror! *(Aside)*

NO. 5 ATTO I continued

TUTTI: *(meno Rig.)* Oh tu che la festa andace hai
turbato,
Da un genio d' inferno qui fosti guidato;
È vano ogni detto, quà t' allontana—
Va, trema, o vegliardo, dell' ira sovrana—
Tu l' hai provocata, più speme non v' è.
Un' ora fatale fu questa per te.
*(Mon. parte fra due alabardieri; tutti gli altra
seguono il Duca in altra, stanza.)*

NO. 7 ATTO I
SCENA VIII
RIG: *(guardando dietro a Sparafucile)*
Pari siamo!—io la lingua, egli ha il pugnale;
L' uomo son io che ride, ei quel che spegne!
Quel vecchio maledivami—
O uomini!—o natura!—
Vil scellerato mi faceste voi!—
Oh rabbia!—esser difforme!—un buffone!—
Non dover, non poter altro che ridere!—
Il retaggio d' ogni uom m' è tolto il pianto!—
Questo padrone mio,
Giovin, giocondo, sì possente, bello
Sonnecchiando mi dice;
Fa ch' io rida, buffone.
Forzarmi deggio, e farlo!—Oh, dannazione!
Odio a voi, cortigiani schernitori!—
Quanta in mordervi ho gioia!—
Se iniquo so, per cagion vostra solo—
Ma in altr' uom quì mi cangio!—
Quel vecchio maledivami!—Tal pensiero

Perchè conturba ognor la mente mia?—
Mi coglierà sventura? Ah no, è folia.
(Apre con chiave, ed entra nel cortile)
*(Detto e Gilda ch' esce dalla casa e si getta nelle
sue braccia.)*

SCENA IX
RIG: Figlia—
GILDA: Mio padre!
RIG: A te d' appresso
Trova sol gioia il core oppresso.
GILDA: Oh quanto amore!
RIG: Mia vita sei!
Senza te in terra qual bene avrei?
(Sospira)
GILDA: Voi sospirate!—che v' ange tanto?
Lo dite a questa povera figlia—
Se v' ha mistero—per lei sia franto—

NO. 5 ACT I continued

ALL, EXCEPT RIG: Rash man, your evil spirit

Has brought you to disturb this feast,
Your words are vain. Away!
The Duke's revenge you raise:
No hope for you remains,
This is your fatal day.
*(Mon. is led away by the soldiers, the others
follow the Duke.)*

NO. 7 ACT I
SCENE VIII
RIG: *(looking after Sparafucile)*
My weapon is my tongue—and his the dagger;
I make the people laugh, he makes them mourn!
We are alike!—That man has cursed me!
Men and nature,
'Tis you that made me wicked;
O rage! to be deformed—and a buffoon!
To be condemned to laugh against my will:
To ask in vain the common gift—of tears!
Alas! my master, young,
And full of mirth,
At every moment says,
Now make me laugh, buffoon.
I must do it. Oh! rage.
I hate you all, vile courtiers!
On you, therefore, my tongue delights to dwell;
For you I am depraved—
But here I am not the same;
That man has cursed me! But why does this
thought
Haunt my mind?
What can I have to fear? No, it's madness.
(He opens and enters.)
*(Enter Gilda from house and throws herself in his
arms.)*

SCENE IX
RIG: My daughter!
GILDA: Father.
RIG: Near to you, alone,
My poor dejected heart returns to joy.
GILDA: My father dear!
RIG: You are my only hope,
What else have I on earth except my Gilda?

GILDA: You sigh! What is the cause of your
affliction?
Tell it to your poor daughter

Ch' ella conosca la sua famiglia.

RIG: Tu non ne hai—
GILDA: Qual nome avete;
RIG: A te che importa?
GILDA: Se non volete
Di voi parlarmi—
RIG: Non uscir mai. (*Interrompendola*)

GILDA: Non vo che al tempio.
RIG: Or ben tu fai.
GILDA: Se non di voi, almen chi sia
Fate ch' io sappia la madre mia.

RIG: Deh non parlare al misero
Del suo perduto bene—
Ella sentia' quell' angelo,
Pietà delle mie pene—
Solo, difforme, povero
Per compassion mi amò.
Morìa—le zolle coprano
Lievi quel capo amato—
Sola or tu resti al misero—
O Dio, sii ringraziato!—
(*Singhiozzande.*)
GILDA: Quanto dolor!—che spremere
Si amaro pianto può?
Padre, non più, calmatevi—
Mi lacerà tal vista—
Il nome vostro ditemi,
Il duol che si v' attrista—
RIG: A che nomarmi?—è inutile!—
Padre, ti sono, e basti—
Me forse al mondo temono,
D'alcuno ho forse gli asti—
Altri mi maledicono—
GILDA: Patria, parenti, amici,
Voi dunque non avete!
RIG: Patria!—parenti!—dici?—
Culto, famiglia, patria,
(*Con effusione.*)
Il mio universo è in te!
GILDA: Ah, se può lieto rendervi,
Gioia è la vita a me!
Già da tre lune son quì venuta,

Nè la cittade ho ancor veduta;
Se il concedete, farlo or potrei—
RIG: Mai!—mai!—uscita, dimmi, unqua sei!
GILDA: No.

NO. 7 ACT I continued

Entrust me with your secrets,
And let me know my family
RIG: Ah! You have none!
GILDA: Your name
RIG: What does it matter to you?
GILDA: If you object to speak
Of our relations—
RIG: Do you ever leave this house? (*Interrupting her.*)
GILDA: I only go to church.
RIG: That's right, my child.
GILDA: If you will not reveal your name or rank,
Ah, let me know, at least, who my mother is.

RIG: Ah, do not awake, I pray,
A memory so sad;
Of my dejected state
She alone had compassion,
Despised, deformed, and poor,
Through pity, she loved me,
She died—ah, may the earth
Lay lightly on her head—
You are my only treasure—
O God! Are you her aid?
(*Sighing.*)
GILDA: Alas, what grief! ah, never
Saw I such bitter tears!
Ah, father, be calm,
Or you will break my heart.
To me reveal your name;
To me your grief impart.
RIG: Why this?—I am your father,
This is enough for you.
I might perhaps be hated,
Or be by others feared.
Alas! I have been cursed!
GILDA: No country, no relations,
No friends, you then possess?
RIG: What do you say, my love?
You are my god, my country,
You are the world to me!

GILDA: If I could see you glad,
I would be happy too.
It has been three months now, since we here arrived,
And nothing I have seen yet of the city.
I wish to see it now, if you will grant it.
RIG: Have you never left this house?
GILDA: Never!

RIG: Guai!
GILDA: (Che dissi?)
RIG: Ben te ne guarda!
(Potrian seguirla, rapirla ancora!
Quì d'un buffone si disonora
La figlia, e se ne ride—Orror!) Olà?
(*Verso la casa.*)

SCENA X
Detti e Giovanna della casa.
GIO: Signor?
RIG: Venendo mi vede alcuno?
Bada, dì il vero—
GIO: Ah no, nessuno.
RIG: Sta ben—la porta che dà al bastione
È sempre chiusa?
GIO: Lo fu e sarà.
RIG: Veglia, o donna, questo fiore (*A Gio.*)
Che a te puro confidài;
Veglia attenta, e non sia mai
Che s' offuschi il suo candor.
Tu dei venti dal furore,
Ch' altri iori hanno piegato,
Lo difendi, e immacolato
Lo ridona al genitor.
GILDA: Quanto affetto!—quali cure!
Che temete, padre mio?
Lassù in cielo, presso Dio
Veglia un angiol protettor.
Da noi stoglie le sventure
Di mia madre il priego santo;
Non fia mai disvelto o franto
Questo a voi diletto fiore.

SCENA XI
Detti ed il Duca in costume borghese dalla strada.
RIG: Alcuno v'é fuori—
(*Apre la porta della Corte, e mentre esce a sulla strada il Duca guizza furtivo nella corte e si nasconde dietro l'albero; gettando a Giovanna una borsa la fa tacer*)
GIL: Cielo!
Sempre novel sospetto—
RIG: (*a Gil. tornando.*)
Vi seguiva alla chiesa mai nessuno!
GIO: Mai.
DUCA: (Rigoletto.)
RIG: Se talor quì picchiano
Guardatevi da aprir—
GIO: Nemmeno al duca?—
RIG: Meno che a tutti a lui—Mia figlia, addio.

NO. 7 ACT I continued

RIG: Mind!
GILDA: (What do I say?)
RIG: Nor must you ever leave it.
(She might be followed, she might be stolen,
And they would laugh at the dishonor
Of a buffoon. Oh shame!) Ho! there!
(*Towards the house.*)

SCENE X
Enter Giovanna from the house.
GIO: Sir?
RIG: Has no one seen me while coming here?
Mind, speak the truth.
GIO: No one.
RIG: That's well! The door that leads to the Ramparts, is it always closed?
GIO: Yes, it has always been so, and always shall.
RIG: Oh, woman, watch over this flower,
Which I trust unto your care;
Be mindful, it may never
Fall the victim of dark snare.
O, save this fragile stem
From the hail and from rain:
As it was to you confided,
May I receive it back again.
GILDA: O, be cheerful, my dear father.
Chase your starting tears away;
There, in heaven, is an angel
Who protects us night and day.
There the prayers of my mother
From all danger keeps us free;
Never, never, from your side,
Never distant will I be.

SCENE XI
The Duke in disguise arrives in the street.
RIG: Some one outside—(*Rigoletto opens the street gate, and whilst he goes out, the Duke slides in, hiding himself behind a tree, and throwing a purse to Giovanna.*)

GILDA: Oh, heavens!
He is always suspicious.
RIG: (*To Gilda, returning.*)
Has any one ever followed you to church?
GIO: No, never. (*Aside.*)
DUKE: (It is Rigoletto.)
RIG: If any one knocks here
You must not open.
GIO: Not even to the Duke?
RIG: Still less to him than others—Child, adieu.

No. 138 Verdi: *Rigoletto* ■ **317**

DUCA: Sua figlia!

GIO: Addio, mia padre. *(S'abbraciano, e Rigoletto parte chiudendosi dietro la porta.)*

* * *

NO. 16 ACT III

SCENA III

Gilda e Rigoletto sulla via, il Duca e Maddalena nel piano terreno.

DUCA: Un dì, se ben rammentomi,
O bella, t'incontrai—
Mi piacque di te chiedere,
E intesi che qui stai.
Or sappi, che d' allora
Sol te quest' alma adora.

MAD: Ah, ah!—e vent' altre appresso
Le scorda forse adesso?—
Ha un' aria il signorino
Da vero libertino—

DUCA: Si?—un mostro son—*(Por abbracciarla.)*

MAD: Lasciatemi, stordito.

DUCA: Ih, che fracasso!

MAD: Stia saggio.

DUCA: E tu sii docile,
Non farmi tanto chiasso.
Ogni saggezza chiudesi
Nel gaudio e nell' amore—
La bella mano candida!—
(Le prende la mano.)

MAD: Scherzate, voi signore.

DUCA: No, no.

MAD: Son brutta.

DUCA: Abbracciami.

MAD: Ebro—

DUCA: D'amore ardente. *(Ridendo)*

MAD: Signor l'indifferente,
Vi piace canzonar?—

DUCA: No, no, ti vo' sposar.

MAD: Ne voglio la parola—

DUCA: Amabile figliuola! *(Ironico.)*

RIG: Ebben?—ti basta ancor?—*(A Gilda che avra tutto osservato ed inteso)*

GIL: Iniquo traditor!

DUCA: Bella figlia dell'amore,
Schiavo son de' vezzi tuoi;
Con un detto soi tu puoi
Le mie pene consolar.
Vieni, e senti del mio core
Il frequente palpitar.

NO. 7 ACT I continued

DUKE: His child!

GILDA: Adieu my father. *(They embrace; and Rigoletto going out, shuts the door after him.)*

* * *

SCENE III

Gilda and Rigoletto on the road. Magdalen and the Duke in the Inn.

DUKE: If I remember well, my pretty girl,
I have seen your face before.
I tried to find your house,
At length I see you here.
Believe that from that time
I loved you to despair.

MAG: And others, score by score,
Do you forget them now?
To tell the truth, good sir,
You are a gay deceiver.

DUKE: Yes, yes, just so.

MAG: Leave me, rude man.

DUKE: Eh! eh! what noise!

MAG: Be quiet.

DUKE: And you be kind,
And do not scream so loud,
For wisdom ever lies
In pleasure and in love.
What pretty hands! how white!
(He takes her by the hand.)

MAG: You like to laugh at me.

DUKE: No, no.

MAG: I know I am not pretty.

DUKE: Kiss me.

MAG: Sir, you are drunk—

DUKE: Yes, drunk of love for you.

MAG: And can you be so unkind,
As thus to laugh at me.

DUKE: I do not joke—I wish to marry you.

MAG: If so, give me your word of honor.

DUKE: You are a charming girl! *(Ironically.)*

RIG: Well then, is this not yet enough?

GIL: The cruel traitor!

DUKE: Lovely woman, of your charms
At your feet the victim see,
But one word, and changed to joy
All my sorrows soon will be.
Yes, be assured, my lady sweet,
This fond heart for you does beat.

NO. 16 ACT III continued

MAD: Ah! ah! rido ben di core,
Chè tai baie costan poco;
Quanto valga il vostro giuoco,
Mel credete, so apprezzar,
Sono avvezza, bel signore,
Ad un simile scherzar.

GIL: Ah, cosi parlar d'amore!
A me pur l'infame ho udito
Infelice cor tradito,
Per angoscia non scoppiar.

RIG: Taci, il piangere non vale; *(A Gil.)*
Ch' ei, mentiva or sei secura—
Taci, e mia sarà la cura
La vendetta d'affrettar.
Pronta fia, sarà fatale;
Io saprollo fulminar.

MAG: Do you take me for a fool,
To think your words are true;
Full well I know what they mean,
I give them their right value,
Jokes like these I often hear,
But I laugh at them, dear sir.

GIL: Thus my heart he did deceive,
Thus the traitor spoke to me.
All my joys, my hopes are gone,
Now my wretched doom I see.

RIG: Hush! your sorrows are all vain,
That he deceived you is now sure—
Hush! it now belongs to me
Dreadful vengeance to procure.
It shall be done quickly, it shall be fatal;
I know how to shoot.

Throughout *Rigoletto,* Verdi incorporates traditional elements of Italian opera (accompanied recitatives, arias, duets, choruses) into an extended whole.

0:00 Preludio: This brief "Prelude" takes the place of a more extended overture. Its somber tone conveys at once that the work to follow will be a tragedy. The "curse" motif figures prominently throughout.

The curtain rises to reveal a scene of dancing, drinking, and revelry in the ballroom of the Duke's palace. This extended opening unit of music consists of eight discrete yet interconnected subsections, in each of which the music underscores the dramatic action:

2:16 The opening dance, played by an onstage band, has the kind of frenzied beat associated with the *galop.*

3:12 When the Duke and one his courtiers enter, the music shifts to a dance that has a lighter texture with emphasis only on beats one and three of a four-beat measure. This change allows the recitative-like patter of the voices to be heard clearly over the orchestra.

3:49 The Duke's first aria (*Questo o quella*) is also the first moment in the opera in which the voice carries the melody completely. The texture here is pointedly homophonic, with the orchestra providing a demure accompaniment. The Duke sings two musically identical strophes (the second begins at m. 48), ending with a vocal cadenza that matches perfectly the boastful nature of his words.

5:31 With the entrance of the Countess of Ceprano, the music changes to a minuet played by an onstage string ensemble. This decidedly old-fashioned dance fits perfectly with the Countess's traditional character. When the Duke leaves with the reluctant countess, Rigoletto and the courtiers ridicule her husband (m. 40). One of the festive dance melodies from the opening returns briefly here. Rigoletto exits and the on-stage ensemble strikes up a *perigordino* (m. 62), a frenzied dance in 6/8 meter.

7:43 The opening galop-like dance resumes briefly with the entrance of Marullo, a courtier who brings "great news." Rigoletto, he reports, has a secret lover.

8:22 The Duke, Rigoletto, and Count Ceprano return, and with them the opening galop-like theme. The Duke rebukes Rigoletto for his excessive jesting about the Count. The chorus of courtiers joins in and in a general frenzy all agree to get their revenge on Rigoletto.

10:16 The music now shifts ominously to accompanied recitative with the entrance of Monterone, whose daughter has earlier been abducted by the Duke. Monterone, in response, lays a curse on the entire court, particularly on Rigoletto, who has taunted him.

Track 17 Act I, Scene 8: Scene and Duet. The "scene" is a monologue in which Rigoletto muses on his deformity, his malicious wit, and his contempt for the Duke and courtiers. In the duet with Gilda, Rigoletto reveals another, more compassionate side to his character. For a detailed diagram of this unit, see Textbook, p. 466.

The final duet within the Duet (m. 243–343) has its own internal structure, a series of variations on a single theme. It follows the traditional pattern of love duets: he sings, she sings, and then they both sing, and in this respect, Verdi adheres to convention. But he also slips in important plot developments within the duet. At m. 279, Rigoletto hears a prowler—the Duke, it turns out—and interrupts himself to launch into an agitated inquisition of Gilda's nursemaid, Giovanna. Thus we have a dramatic dialogue in the middle of the duet (Rigoletto: "No one has followed her from church?" Giovanna (lying): "Never!" and so on). Meanwhile, the Duke himself has been listening in on all this and realizes that the woman he has been pursuing (Gilda) is the daughter of his court jester (Rigoletto), and he interjects a few asides to express his astonishment at this revelation. With his fears calmed, Rigoletto resumes his duet with Gilda, who sings a glorious descant to his original melody (m. 303). The protracted farewell provides the traditional cabaletta, an extended concluding section that accelerates as it nears the end of this very long unit of music.

139 Tristan und Isolde (1859)
Richard Wagner (1813–1883)

139a Prelude

CD12, Track 3

Book p. 454

4:02.64

7:32.13

Note: This edition is a piano-vocal reduction of Wagner's original score for voices and orchestra.

326 ■ No. 139 Wagner: *Tristan und Isolde*

0:07.55

1:13.38

2:05

8:06

The Prelude (overture) begins with what will prove to be the most important musical idea over the course of the drama, one associated with the love potion Tristan and Isolde will drink in Act I (see Example 2).

The extended dissonance on the so-called "Tristan chord" (on the downbeat of m. 2) and its upward chromatic "resolution" (m. 3) convey the sense of painful yearning that dominates love's longing. The formal structure of the prelude as a whole does not follow sonata form or any other conventional pattern. Instead, Wagner goes on to fragment, extend, transpose, invert, and otherwise manipulate the opening idea in a variety of ways. The rising minor chromatic third first heard in m. 2–3 assumes special importance. Wagner manipulates a fragment of this theme (Example 3a, first measure; Example 3b) by using repetition, harmonic variation, melodic variation, and silence to enrich each successive statement. The Prelude as a whole follows no established convention of large-scale form. Instead, the music seems to propel itself forward through a series of constant transformations. For example, the rising three-note figure that first appears in the cellos in m. 17 (see Example 3, m. 2) represents a metamorphosis of the rising minor chromatic third from m. 2–3. This new idea, in turn is further fragmented and manipulated in m. 36–37. The orchestra, all the while, builds gradually in size and volume, reaching a high point of sorts with the fortissimo statement of yet another version of the cello's theme at m. 74. But a crashing dissonance (m. 83) turns out to be the true climax, however, for it ushers in a return to the quiet tension of the opening (m. 85). There is no sense of resolution here: the music closes pianissimo and leads without a pause into the opening scene of Act I.

Example 2 The "love potion" motif, with the "Tristan chord" highlighted

"Tristan chord"

In the excerpt from Act II, Isolde and her maidservant Brangaene await the onset of night; Tristan has left with King Mark's hunting party, but at a signal from Isolde—the moment she extinguishes the torch on the castle's ramparts—Tristan will return. The musical transformations of the love potion motif continue throughout, as for example when Brangaene laments having substituted a love potion for what was supposed to be a death potion (m. 351–353), and then again more tellingly shortly afterward (m. 380–382), when Isolde explains that it was the power of love that caused the potion to transform itself. Here, underneath Isolde's declamation (beginning at m. 385), the orchestra spins out a series of thematic variants based on the characteristic rising chromatic third we first heard in the work's opening measures. Isolde now views the love potion quite differently, and the orchestra reflects this by presenting the motif within the guise of a softer, more lyrical tone. In Wagnerian terms, Isolde gives voice to what the orchestra is already expressing through music alone.

The motif known as "love's longing" (Example 4) represents yet another manipulation of the rising chromatic third. Here, the melodic trajectory is reversed: the chromatic line moves downward and is supported by a clearly outlined triadic base. The feeling here is more confident, more directional, as befits the dramatic situation. This motif dominates the tension that builds toward Tristan's return. Still another metamorphosis of this motif (Example 5) emerges when Tristan finally arrives: the theme becomes ecstatic, rising in its opening to a high note before descending, rather than descending from the very start. Such changes, subtle but effective, have led more than one commentator to accord this idea a separate identity, associating it with the idea of "bliss"—which is of course the desired consequence of longing. The musical and dramatic parallels function in tandem.

Another prominent *Leitmotiv* in *Tristan and Isolde* is associated with death (*Tod* in the German text). Like the "love potion" motif, the "death" motif (Example 6) is chromatic and harmonically unusual. (Wagner often used chromatic themes or unusual harmonic progressions to evoke conditions of pain, such as love and death.) Although the "death" motif manifests itself in many different ways, its characteristic harmonic feature is the juxtaposition of two otherwise distant chords (such as A♭ major and A major, as in Example 6) combined with a distinctive dotted rhythm.

Having established these and other motifs in the listener's mind (conscious or unconscious), Wagner is free to use it in any number of ways, some of them obvious, some of them

Example 3 Subsequent transformations of the "love potion" motif

(a)

(b)

Example 4 "Love's longing"

Example 5 "Bliss"

Example 6 "Death"

Tod - ge - weih - tes Haupt! Tod - ge - weih - tes Herz!

Death-destined head! Death-destined heart!

not. Near the end of Act II Scene 1, for example, at the moment when Isolde extinguishes her torch, thereby giving Tristan the signal to leave the hunting party and return to the castle, Wagner embeds the "death" motif in the orchestra (beginning at m. 485). (The texture is so thick at this point that the motif is not evident in the piano reduction of the score in the Anthology.) What is the connection between this moment and death? Once Tristan returns, the lovers will consummate their passion, which in turn will lead to their deaths. By linking the extinguishing of the torch to the "death" motif, Wagner is telling us, in musical terms, that the act carries ultimately fatal consequences.

The labels we have been using to identify these Leitmotivs, although useful for analyzing Wagner's music, can lead us to think of them (incorrectly) as fixed entities, both musically and in terms of their dramatic associations. Probably for this reason, Wagner himself almost never explicitly identified any of these themes. It would be tedious, pointless, and ultimately impossible to ascribe an individual name to every different manifestation of every motif, in any event. More important is to recognize how Wagner works his Leitmotivs into an ever-evolving web of complementary and contrasting musical and dramatic relationships that can sustain a work lasting many hours in performance.

The performance: Improvisation and embellishment have never played an important role in Wagner's. The demands on the singers' voices are nevertheless considerable. In *Tristan und Isolde,* the two main characters remain on stage for very long stretches at a time: vocal endurance is a prerequiste of great Wagnerian voices. They must also be able to project through the sound of a large orchestra that is itself richly textured. Beyond all this, singers must negotiate a dauntingly wide register. This is particularly true of sopranos (see, for example, Isolde's high C two octaves above middle C in m. 589). The recording here, made during a live performance at Bayreuth in 1966, features Birgit Nilsson (1918–2005), the greatest Wagnerian soprano of her generation.

140 The Pirates of Penzance (1879)
William S. Gilbert (1836–1911) and
Arthur Sullivan (1842–1900)

CD12, Track 5
Book p. 461

Note: This edition is a piano-vocal reduction of Sullivan's original score for voices and orchestra.

1:43.5

Gilbert and Sullivan's operettas—plays with significant quantities of sung music—draw heavily on the principal forms of opera, with numbers that are easily recognizable as arias, duets, ensembles, and even accompanied recitatives. At the same time, their works manage to poke fun these very same conventions. The sustained tremolo in the opening recitative of this scene from *The Pirates of Penzance,* for example, suggests a matter of grave importance, and the pirates are indeed cowed when Mabel informs them that her father is major general. The ensuing aria ("I am the Very Model of a Modern Major General") parodies the kind of rapid-fire declamation so popular in Italian opera (see, for example, Figaro's aria, Anthology No. 2/137). This "patter song" is all the more amusing coming from a major general rather than a servant.

Performance notes: The performance here is from the D'Oyly Carte Opera Company production recorded in 1949. Established by Richard D'Oyly Carte in 1875 and in operation until 2003, this troupe gave the premiere performances of many of Gilbert and Sullivan's most celebrated operettas. Every generation of this company has interpreted these works in its own way, but the degree of historical continuity in a single institution remains remarkable.

141   Vorwärts! (1848)
Clara Wieck Schumann (1819–1896)

CD12, Track 7
Book p. 462

*)Eine Variante des Schlusses ab Takt 37
ist auf S. 11 abgedruckt.

No. 141 Schumann: *Vorwärts!* ■ 345

37 A Variante

durch des To- des Pein! Wer den Him- mel will ge- win- nen, muß ein rech- ter Kämp-fer

durch des To- des Pein! Wer den Him- mel will ge- win- nen, muß ein rech- ter Kämp-fer

42 A

sein,__ wer den Him- mel will ge- win- nen, wer den Him- mel will __ ge- winnen, muß ein

muß ein rech- ter, ein

sein,__ wer den Him- mel will ge- win- nen, muß ein rech- ter, ein

48 A

rech- ter Kämp-fer sein, wer den Him- mel will ge- win- nen, muß ein rech-ter Kämp-fer sein.

rech- ter Kämp-fer sein, wer den Him- mel will ge- win- nen, muß ein rech-ter Kämp-fer sein.

1. Lass das Träumen, lass das Zagen,	Leave the dreaming and hesitation behind,
Unermüdet wandre fort!	Without fatigue, go forward!
Will die Kraft dir schier versagen,	If you simply run out of energy,
"Vorwärts!" ist das rechte Wort.	"Forward!" is the right word.
2. Darfst nicht weilen, wenn die Stunde	You may not dally, if the day
Rosen dir entgegenbringt,	Brings you roses,
Wenn dir aus des Meeres Grunde	Or if from the depths of the ocean
Die Sirene lockend singt.	The siren sings seductively to you.
3. Vorwärts, vorwärts! Im Gesange	Forward, forward! In song
Ringe mit dem Schmerz der Welt,	Wrestle with the suffering of the world,
Bis auf deine heisse Wange	Until on your hot cheek
Goldner Strahl von oben fällt,	A golden ray from above should fall,
4. Bis der Kranz, der dichtbelaubte,	Until the crown, thickly woven,
Schattig deine Stirn umwebt,	wraps itself with shadows around your head,
Bis verklärend überm Haupte	Until above your head transfigured
Dir des Geistes Flamme schwebt.	The flame of the spirit hovers before you.
5. Vorwärts drum durch Feindes Zinnen,	Forward, then, through the enemy's lines,
Vorwärts durch des Todes Pein,	Forward through the pain of death,
Wer den Himmel will gewinnen,	Whoever would gain entry to heaven
Muss ein rechter Kämpfer sein!	Must be a true fighter!

--Transl. MEB

A note on the edition: This edition includes a variant version of the work's closing measures (beginning at m. 47). The recording presents the standard version as given on p. 345.

Singing had always been part of most religious observance in Europe; now a new repertoire of a cappella, secular four-part songs was written expressly for amateur small choruses that gathered on a regular basis to perform. If this practice's *raison d'etre* was primarily social at first, it was soon taken far more seriously by some, who formed singing clubs (*Singverein*) with strong community ties, performing in concerts and competitions and opening a new market for publishers.

It was for such a group that Clara Wieck Schumann wrote *Drei gemischte Chöre* ("Three Mixed Choruses," to texts by Emanuel Geibel, 1848), from which "Vorwärts" ("Forward") is taken. The text was written in 1840, when rumblings against post-Napoleonic governments had begun. Schumann's setting, composed as revolution appeared imminent, is full of fervor; rather than simply repeat the music for all five strophes, Schumann structures the music as $ABA^1B^1A^2$; the repeated final phrase ("Wer den Himmel will gewinnen/ Muss ein rechter Kämpfer sein!") features a climactic high note on "Himmel" (heaven) and a brief staggered entry for further emphasis prior to the close of the piece. The choruses remained in manuscript and were not published until 1988, which kept Schumann out of personal political difficulty during her lifetime.

142 Virga Jesse floruit (1885)
Anton Bruckner (1824–1896)

CD12, Track 8

Book p. 466

1:45.6

al - le - lu - ja.

al - le - lu - ja.

falsetto
lu - ja, al - le - lu - ja, al - le - lu - ja, al - le - lu - ja.

- ja, al - le - lu - ja.

Virga Jesse floruit:
Virgo Deum et hominem genuit:
pacem Deus reddidit,
in se reconcilians ima summis.
Alleluja.

The rod of Jesse blossomed:
A virgin brought forth [both] God and man:
God restored peace,
in Himself reconciling the lowest [and] highest.
Alleluia.

The text of this motet is the Alleluia of any Mass for the Feast of the Blessed Virgin Mary during Paschal time. It refers to Isaiah's Old Testament prophecy that an offshoot of Jesse (the father of King David) would blossom and give birth to the Messiah. The strict four-part counterpoint and a cappella setting suggest at first a motet in the style of the late Renaissance. But the unusual harmonic turn and crescendo on the first *floruit* ("flourished") in m. 7–9 reveal this to be a work of the Caecilian movement, an attempt by various composers of the 19th century to recreate—without imitating precisely—the style of Renaissance polyphony. The linear chromaticism, the sudden harmonic turns, and the wide melodic leaps in the individual voice parts are all typical of the late 19th century.

143 An der schönen blauen Donau,
Op. 314 (On the Beautiful Blue Danube)
(Original orchestral version reduced for piano) (1867)
Johann Strauss, Jr. (1825–1899)

CD12, Track 9
Book p. 468

2:50.18

3:52.19

No. 143 Strauss: *An der schönen blauen Donau*   ■   **351**

4:49.54

6:01.08

7:59.34

No. 143 Strauss: *An der schönen blauen Donau* ■ **353**

The form of Strauss's "On the Beautiful Blue Danube" is typical of many dances from the late 19th century. It consists of an extended introduction followed by a series of individual waltzes (numbered 1, 2, 3, etc.), most in binary form, each with its own thematic idea, and some with their own introductions (marked "Intrada" in the score). This modular structure allowed ensembles to repeat any individual waltz as often as needed. At the same time, Strauss was careful to integrate the sequence of dances into a coherent whole. The introduction (notated in A major but heard as the dominant of D) establishes the tonic key of D major for most of the waltzes. The fourth waltz modulates to F major for the sake of harmonic variety, and an extended coda brings the work to a close in the tonic and reprises the theme of the opening waltz. Typically for dance music, each of the individual waltzes within *An der schönen blauen Donau* is built on units of four or eight measures, which join to create larger units of 16 or 32 measures. This kind of rhythmic and structural predictability was essential for the function of social dance and would become the basis for many forms of dance or dance-related genres in the 20th century, including ragtime, the blues, and even rock and roll.

0:35

1:04

1:35

No. 144 Sousa: *King Cotton* ■ **355**

CD12, Track 11
Book p. 470

Le café (Danse Arabe)

The march, like dance music, was written to coordinate physical movement—in this case, of soldiers. Like Strauss's waltzes, Sousa's marches are invariably modular in structure, built on units of 4, 8, 16, and 32 measures, and in performance, each unit can be repeated as often as desired. In *King Cotton,* every unit marked by a repeat sign consists of 16 measures, with an extended closing section of 32 (16 + 16 measures). For each of these, Sousa wrote out altered orchestrations and added new contrapuntal lines to be played the second time around; note, for example, the added trombone line that stands out prominently in the repetition of the last half of the march's last unit. Tonal closure is not an issue of great concern in the march repertory: Sousa's marches often begin in one key and end in another. *King Cotton,* starts in the key of E♭, and ends in A♭ major. This "conductor score" is really a short score, in which the original orchestration is reduced to three staves for use by band directors.

[Strike] the membrane with the thumb.

Le thé (Danse Chinoise)

Trépak (Danse Russe)

In the last third of the century, Tchaikovsky emerged as the preeminent composer of ballet music. His lyricial melodies and rich orchestrations combined to make his *Swan Lake* (1876), *Sleeping Beauty* (1889), and *The Nutcracker* (1892) among the most enduringly popular works of their kind. *The Nutcracker,* based on the well-known story by E. T. A. Hoffmann, combines a real-life plot with fairy-tale fantasy. In Act I, a mysterious inventor named Drosselmeyer gives a young girl, Clara, a magical nutcracker as a present. At night the nutcracker comes to life and leads an army of toy soldiers into battle with an army of mice. When Clara saves the Nutcracker's life, he transforms into a handsome young man. In Act II, the transformed Nutcracker takes Clara on a magical journey that ends in the Land of Flowers, where they meet the Sugar Plum Fairy. The *divertissements* of Act II allow Tchaikovsky to construct a series of loosely connected vignettes, each of which presents the characteristic sound (or what at least was believed at the time to be the characteristic sound) of a variety of exotic lands. In "Le café" ("Coffee"), Tchaikovsky uses a drone-like bass beneath a trio of single-reed instruments (English horn and two clarinets), muted strings, and tambourine to evoke images of Arabia. "Le thé" ("Tea") takes us to China, for which Tchaikovsky creates a very different kind of sound based on the contrast of flutes and piccolo against pizzicato strings, all inflected melodies based on a pentatonic or quasi-pentatonic scale, traditionally associated (at least in the Western mind) with the music of China. The initial statement of the pizzicato figure in the strings, for example, is constructed solely on the pitches F-A-B♭-C-D. The ensuing "Trépak" takes up the rhythms of this characteristically Russian dance. The musical exoticism of all these dances held particular appeal for audiences of the late 19th century at a time when the European world was claiming dominion over vast portions of the earth.

146 Symphony No. 4 in E minor, Op. 98,
fourth movement (finale) (1885)
Johannes Brahms (1833–1897)

CD13, Track 1
Book p. 475

0:29.14

1:01.57

1:34.4

2:36.46

3:18.60

5:17.4

6:52

7:30.46

7:53.32

8:29.7

9:02.37

9:55.9

10:15.22

The finale of Brahms's last symphony is an enormous set of variations on a theme. On one level, the structure of this movement is quite simple: it is a series of 30 variations, each eight measures long and based on the same eight-measure theme (see examples below). Within this relatively simple—one might be tempted to say restrictive—framework, Brahms introduces a stunning variety of thematic ideas, textures, harmonies, and colors. The theme is derived from the ostinato finale of Bach's Cantata No. 150, a work that Brahms knew well.

Example 7 Ostinato theme of Bach, Cantata no. 150, finale (transposed)

Example 8 Brahms's ostinato bass for the finale of his Symphony no. 4

Bach's ostinato theme is not particularly distinctive: it fills in the interval of a fifth and ends with an octave leap on the dominant, which in turn sets up the repetition of the theme. Brahms extends the theme to eight measures (one note per measure), moves the melodic idea to the uppermost voice, and adds a striking dissonance by sharpening the second iteration of the fourth scale degree (A♯). He further deviates from Bach's theme by ending on the first scale degree. The resulting harmonic closure increases the challenge of composing a continuous movement from a string of such sequences, but it is a challenge Brahms confronts with zeal. By the time we reach the middle of this movement, we have to remind ourselves that it is in fact a set of variations on a theme. The division between variations 6 and 7 (m. 49–56 and 57–64), is almost imperceptible even when we listen for it. The movement nevertheless holds consistently to the repeating eight-measure structure all the way through Variation 30. Only the coda, beginning in m. 253 after a few introductory measures, is freely composed.

Within this self-imposed structure of variations on a theme, Brahms integrates another formal principle, that of sonata form. In a strict sense, the movement is not in sonata form because it lacks the essential modulation to a secondary key. Still, there is an unmistakable sense of transition in variations 10 and 11 (m. 81–88, 89–96) and a clear change of mood with variation 12 (m. 97–104): the meter changes, the music is marked *dolce* for the first time, and the timbre of the solo flute dominates the substantially thinned texture. The impression of change is reinforced in variation 13 (m. 105–112) with a shift to E major. Variation 16 marks the onset of what corresponds to the development, and variation 24 sounds very much like the beginning of a recapitulation. The material after variation 30, as noted above, constitutes a freely composed coda.

With this finale of his last symphony, Brahms seems to be reminding the musical world that old forms are capable of rejuvenation, that it is possible to search for the new without abandoning tradition entirely. With its ostensibly simple construction, this movement is firmly rooted in tradition, but in its harmony, orchestration, and sense of flow, it is distinctly progressive.

("From the New World"), Largo (1893)
Antonin Dvořák (1841–1904)

CD12, Track 14
Book p. 479

8:02.20

No. 147 Dvořák: *Symphony No. 9 in E minor*　　■　**389**

8:57

No. 147 Dvořák: *Symphony No. 9 in E minor*   ■ **391**

In his Symphony No. 9, Dvořák synthesizes the traditions of the Old and New Worlds. Structurally, the work follows the standard pattern of four movements: a sonata-form first movement with an extended slow introduction; a pastoral slow movement (the Largo); a fast, dance-like third movement in triple meter; and a rousing finale that breaks through from minor to major. Within each of these individual movements, however, Dvořák incorporates what he considered to be characteristic elements of indigenous American music. The principal theme of the Largo, for example (beginning at m. 7), is largely pentatonic—that is, based on a scale of only five notes. Although frequently associated with the music of East Asia, pentatonic scales figure large in many traditional ("folk") idioms of the West as well, and when Europeans like Dvořák heard Native Americans making music, they tended to hear the melodies as characteristically pentatonic. The opening phrase on the English horn (which sounds a fifth lower than notated) uses primarily the pitches D♭, E♭, F, A♭, and B♭. The C♮ that first appears in m. 11 functions as a leading tone to the tonic, but the scale of the melody pointedly avoids the fourth scale degree in the key of D♭ (that is, G♭), thereby lending a strongly pentatonic coloring to the theme. The melody of the contrasting section in C♯ minor (beginning at m. 46), played on flutes and oboes, is also constructed on a pentatonic scale (C♯-D♯-E-G♯-B), again omitting the fourth scale degree (F♯).

The orchestration and harmonization of both these melodies contribute to the pastoral tone of the movement. The English horn and oboe are both reed instruments and thus connected, at least indirectly, to the shepherd's reed pipe; the flute, too, is an instrument associated with the idealized serenity of the countryside. The drone bass underneath both melodies, reminiscent of a bagpipe, further contributes to this air of calm. But pastoral scenes are almost inevitably disrupted at some point, and Dvořák's Largo holds true to form: the C♯ minor section introduces a dark and at times threatening tone to the whole. The extended section over a "walking bass" (beginning at m. 54) includes still more pentatonically inflected melodies. The idea in the flute incorporates the so-called Scotch snap, a short note on the accented beat followed by a longer note. In m. 60, for example, the sixteenth note in the flute is followed by a dotted quarter tied to a half, emphasizing rhythmically the melodic absence of the fourth scale degree in the melodic fragment (E-F♯-G♯-B-C♯). Yet another important interruption, a lively major-mode section (beginning at m. 90) leads to a portentous reference back to the main theme of the first movement (m. 96)—Dvořák carefully integrates all four movements of the symphony—before the original mood of calm is restored with the return of the English horn theme in the tonic (m. 101).

Dvořák himself pointed to Henry Wadsworth Longfellow's *Song of Hiawatha* as the source of inspiration for this movement, though it is not altogether clear whether Dvořák meant a particular passage in this long poem or the mood of the poem as a whole. For many listeners, however, including even those attending the premiere of this symphony, Dvořák's work was primarily based on what they called "Negro melodies." "The composer has not taken the external forms of plantation music," one critic of the time noted, "but has used his own themes suggested by the southern music. Now and then the motifs and the rhythms strongly suggest the origin of the symphony."[1] These connections were reinforced in the public mind in 1922 when the American composer William Arms Fischer (1861–1948), who had studied with Dvořák, set the Largo's English horn theme to a text he had written in the style

[1]James Creelman, "Dvořák's Negro Symphony," *Pall Mall Budget,* 21 June 1894; reproduced in *Dvořák and His World,* ed. Michael Beckerman (Princeton, NJ: Princeton University Press, 1993), p. 179.

of a Negro spiritual ("Goin' home, goin' home, I'm a-goin' home / Quiet like, some still day, I jes' goin' home"). With these words, the melody became the basis for any number of subsequent arrangements, and to this day many concert-goers believe that Dvořák had in fact used an old spiritual as the basis for the Largo of his "New World" Symphony. That the two traditions of American music Dvořák considered so potentially fruitful—Native American and African-American music—should have become so thoroughly fused in the public mind testifies to the composer's ability to capture a spirit that was somehow "American" without being either specific or immediately identifiable.

148 Symphony No. 1 in D Major,
third movement (1888)
Gustav Mahler (1860–1911)

CD13, Track 2
Book p. 483

1:02.2

2:10

4:00.26

4:58.42

No. 148 Mahler: *Symphony No. 1 in D Major* ■ 397

7:02

The third movement of Mahler's First Symphony careens wildly from the beautiful to the grotesque, the sincere to the ironic. Mahler himself once suggested that the entire movement was inspired by a well-known illustration (see p. 483 of the Textbook) showing wild animals bearing a hunter to his grave. By writing a funeral march into his symphony, Mahler is of course directly linking it to the funeral march in the second movement of Beethoven's "Eroica." But the ironic tone of this music, inspired by a grotesque ceremony in which the hunted bury the hunter, mocks the somberness of the earlier work. The solemn tread of the timpani in the opening measures of the movement, combined with its slow tempo, low register, and minor mode all combine to announce that this will be a funeral march befitting the slow movement of a symphony. The instrument playing the melody is a solo double bass, and it is playing in a torturously high range for that instrument. The tone is not deep and resonant, but pinched and forced. Odder still, the melody turns out be a minor-mode variant of the children's tune "Frère Jacques" (or "Bruder Martin," as it is known in German-speaking lands). A children's play song in minor in the slow movement of a symphony? We can begin to understand why so many contemporary critics found Mahler's music perplexing and at times exasperating.

Still other critics (many of them motivated by anti-Semitism) criticized the passage immediately following for its "Jewish" or "eastern" qualities. The sound world evoked here (beginning in m. 39) is that of the *Klezmorim,* the professional Jewish musicians of eastern Europe—what we refer to today as Klezmer music, characterized by a steady "oompah" sound in the bass (here, in low strings, bass drum, and cymbals) and rhythmically free winds above. Chromatic passages in thirds, exaggerated accents, repeated half-steps back and forth, and the prominence of the shrill-sounding E♭ clarinet all contribute to what many critics dismissed as the music of peasants, not suited to the lofty realm of the symphony. After a brief return of the "Bruder Martin" theme (m. 71), the mood shifts yet again, introducing a passage of lyrical beauty accompanied now by the harp (beginning in m. 83). Mahler uses here a melody from a song he himself had written several years before entitled "The Two Blue Eyes of My Beloved," and the tone is decidedly sincere: the composer indicates that this section is to be played "very simply and unadorned, like a folk melody," in contrast to the Klezmer-like passages, which he directs at one point to be played "like a parody" (m. 45).

All these contrasts are intentionally jarring, and Mahler uses them to drive home his belief that a symphony can and should encompass the banal and mundane as well as the beautiful. The contrast between the funeral marches of Beethoven's Third Symphony and Mahler's First Symphony manifests the enormous changes music had experienced in less than a century. Beethoven's music is earnest, sincere, unselfconscious; Mahler's by contrast, combines hauntingly beautiful melodies with passages that fairly drip with irony. Mahler's subsequent symphonies manifest similar contrasts of tone, at times deadly serious, at times light-hearted and remote. All of his symphonies are large-scale works: unlike Mendelssohn, Schumann, and Brahms, he built on the monumental aspect of the genre as embodied above all in Beethoven's Ninth Symphony, but also in Schubert's "Great" C Major Symphony, D. 944, and the symphonies of Bruckner.

149 Prélude à l'Après-midi d'un faune
(1894)

Claude Debussy (1862–1918)

CD13, Track 3
Book p. 520

0:43.88

1:35.65

2:48.24

3:16.46

4:33.62

■ No. 149 Debussy: *Prélude à l'Après-midi d'un faune*

No. 149 Debussy: *Prélude à l'Après-midi d'un faune* ■ **413**

6:21.65

7:39.70

Debussy's "Prelude to an Afternoon of a Faun" was inspired by a symbolist poem, Stéphane Mallarmé's *L'Après-midi d'un faune* ("Afternoon of a Faun," 1876). Evocative and at times obscure, Mallarmé's poem captures the ruminations of a mythological faun, a half-man, half-goat who remembers—or did he only dream about?—his erotically charged encounter with a pair of wood nymphs. The opening line reads: "Those nymphs, I want to make them permanent," and the rest of the poem floats between dream and consciousness. Illusion and reality are indistinguishable.

Critics have drawn many indirect and a few direct connections between Mallarmé's poetry and Debussy's music. The faun's instrument is traditionally the flute, and it is this instrument that opens Debussy's work. The languorous chromatic line falls and rises like the faun's own fantasy. Debussy himself was evasive about further particulars, however, stating merely that his piece conveyed "a general impression of the poem, because if music were to follow more closely it would run out of breath, like a dray horse competing for the Grand Prize with a thoroughbred . . ." Yet the consistent opposition between flute and strings and the points of structural articulation (m. 30–31, 37, 55, 80, 94) resonates subtly with both the design and content of Mallarmé's poem.

It is also unclear why Debussy called this the "Prelude" to the faun's afternoon. At one point he had announced a forthcoming work entitled *Prélude, interludes et paraphrase finale pour l'Après-midi d'un faune,* and it would seem that the first of these, the prelude, was the only movement the composer actually completed. In a way, though, the title fits the poetry, which holds many mysteries that cannot be rationally explained.

For traditionally minded listeners of the late 19th century, Debussy's *Prélude à l'Après-midi d'un faune* was an enigma. They found the lack of clearly defined themes, the successions of seventh chords (m. 48–49), and the parallel fifths (m. 102) primitive in the worst sense of the word. Almost thirty years after the work's premiere, Camille Saint-Saëns (1835–1921), one of the leading French composers of his generation, wrote privately to a friend that he could make little sense of the work, accusing it of cultivating an "absence of style." But others found in this "absence of style" an inspiration, a new approach to music that opened the door to writing in a manner that was decidedly modern. While no single work can be said to represent birth of modernism, Debussy's *Prélude à l'Après-midi d'un faune* epitomizes the assault on traditional elements and attitudes that characterizes a great deal of music written at the end of the 19th century and at the beginning of the 20th.

Debussy

CD13, Track 4
Book p. 521

1:00.28

1:48.34

Debussy's *Voiles,* published in the first book of Preludes for the Piano (1910), is full of parallel octaves and fifths, and its harmonies are obstinately nondirectional. Its supple rhythms add to a sensation of constant fluidity, as does its form. Although the work follows an ABA pattern in its broadest outlines, with the A section returning at m. 58, critics disagree as to whether the B section starts at m. 23, 37, or 55. Here as elsewhere, Debussy's music is delightfully ambiguous. Even the title has two possible meanings: "sails" or "veils."

More important, *Voiles* also illustrates the increasing use of nontraditional scale forms in the early decades of the 20th century. Debussy constructs the melodic ideas of this work primarily from whole-tone and pentatonic scales:

- Based on six notes, each a whole tone apart, the whole-tone scale subverts some of the most basic elements of diatonic harmony: it cannot be used to construct major and minor triads, and it permits a few seventh chords. In *Voiles,* Debussy uses a whole tone scale in the outer sections. Here again, the effect is one of a freely floating tonality with no clear center—very much in keeping with the work's evocative title ("Sails" or "Veils"). The opening figure is based on the scale built on C, but with no half-steps.

- Although frequently associated with East Asian music, pentatonic scales—scales based on five notes—are found in many traditional ("folk") idioms of the West as well. Debussy uses one such scale in the inner section of *Voiles,* beginning at m. 42.

Mikrokosmos, Book 4, No. 101:
Diminished Fifth (between 1932 and 1939)
Béla Bartók (1881–1945)

CD13, Track 5
Book p. 523

Bartók's *Mikrokosmos* is a set of 153 etude-like works issued in six volumes between 1926 and 1937. The short piece entitled "Diminished Fifth," which explores various compositional possibilities of this interval, is based on the octatonic scale, a scale that alternates between half and whole steps and contains within itself all possible intervals, from the minor second to the major seventh. "Diminished Fifth" repeatedly juxtaposes two tetrachords (four-note units) that together make up the octatonic scale outlined here:

Example 9 Octatonic scale used in m. 1–5 of Béla Bartók, *Diminished Fifth*

Because of its symmetrical construction and strict alternation between half and whole steps, an octatonic scale tends to subvert the idea of a tonal center.

152 The Cage (1906)
Charles Ives (1874–1954)

CD13, Track 6
Book p. 524

NOTE:- All notes not marked with sharp or flat are natural.

Ives's *The Cage* is an early attempt to write using quartal harmonies, that is, chords built on the interval of a fourth rather than a third. The unsettling text, about a leopard pacing in his cage, receives an appropriately repetitive and unsettling melody whose relentless up-and-down progression creates a kind of "cage" in its own right. The accompaniment provides little sense of direction, at least not within the expected conventions of triadic harmony. This brief song, in effect, is in no key at all. Notice, too, the absence of any meter or bar lines.

153 The Things Our Fathers Loved (1917)
Ives

CD13, Track 7

Book p. 524

This song, written to a text by the composer himself, plays with traditional harmony by stringing together a series of tunes from popular songs but joining and harmonizing them in an extremely unusual manner, often in the "wrong" key. *Dixie,* at the very beginning, merges imperceptibly into *My Old Kentucky Home,* followed by *On the Banks of the Wabash* (at the words "I hear the organ on the Main Street corner"), then the hymn tune *Nettleton* ("Aunt Sarah humming Gospels"), and *The Battle Cry of Freedom* ("The village cornet band, playing in the square. The town's Red, White, and Blue"), and finally *In the Sweet Bye and Bye* ("Now! Hear the songs!"). The harmonizations of these tunes—all of them familiar to Ives's contemporaries—create a strange sense of distance. The familiar becomes unfamiliar, and the way in which one melodic fragment flows into the next, always to words from a different source, seems very much in keeping with the literary technique of the stream of consciousness developed by the modernist author James Joyce. The net result is a song that insists on its modernity even while celebrating (and quoting from) songs of the past.

CD13, Track 8

Book p. 524

NOTE: *The publisher of this music refused permission to reproduce more than two pages of the score. We regret the subsequent omission of the remaining three pages of the score here. The work is recorded in its entirety on the anthology of recordings accompanying this textbook.*

Ives's *The Unanswered Question* directly juxtaposes traditional and nontraditional harmonies. The solo trumpet and the small ensemble of flutes seem to occupy an entirely different musical sphere from the strings. The strings speak in slow, measured, chorale-like tones, using the tonal language of conventional triads. Dissonance in the strings is carefully controlled and resolved: the entire string part, in fact, looks and sounds almost like a student essay in species counterpoint. The solo trumpet, by contrast, repeatedly poses a five-note figure that implies no harmonic center at all (B♭-C♯-E-E♭-C, or, in some instances, ending with a B♮ instead of a C). The flutes, in turn, are even more tonally diffuse and grow rhythmically more independent. The work ends with a serene, perfect authentic G-major triad, yet the sensation it creates is not one of resolution.

In his foreword to the score of *The Unanswered Question,* Ives gave some hint as to the symbolism behind these contrasting elements:

> The strings play *ppp* throughout with no change in tempo. They are to represent "The Silence of the Druids—Who Know, See and Hear Nothing." The trumpet intones "The Perennial Question of Existence," and states it in the same tone of voice each time. But the hunt for "The Invisible Answer" undertaken by the flutes and other human beings, becomes gradually more active, faster and louder through an *animando* [animatedly] to a *con fuoco* [with fire]. This part need not be played in the exact time position indicated. It is played in somewhat of an impromptu way; if there be no conductor, one of the flute players may direct their playing. "The Fighting Answerers," as the time goes on, and after a "secret conference," seem to realize a futility, and begin to mock "The Question" —the strife is over for the moment. After they disappear, "The Question" is asked for the last time, and "The Silences" are heard beyond in "Undisturbed Solitude."

CD13, Track 9
Book p. 528

155 Le Sacre du printemps, excerpt (1913)
Igor Stravinsky (1882–1971)

■ No. 155 Stravinsky: *Le Sacre du printemps*

430 ■ No. 155 Stravinsky: *Le Sacre du printemps*

ВЕСЕННІЯ ГАДАНІЯ.
ПЛЯСКИ ЩЕГОЛИХЪ.

LES AUGURES PRINTANIERS.
DANSES DES ADOLESCENTES.

3:08.39

No. 155 Stravinsky: *Le Sacre du printemps*   ■   **431**

3:32.13

3:45.19

The scenario of Stravinsky's ballet *Le Sacre du printemps* ("The Rite of Spring," subtitled "Pictures from Pagan Russia") centers on a pre-Christian ritual that welcomes the coming of spring and offers in thanks to the gods a human sacrifice—primitive and uncivilized to be sure, but consequently all the more elemental and powerful. By rejecting traditional harmonic progressions, timbres, and above all rhythms, Stravinsky was able to create a score that reflected the same kind of raw, elemental relationship between man and nature that is represented on stage through the story of the dance. Stravinsky elevates the role of rhythm—the most basic of all musical elements—in a number of ways, sometimes through complexity, sometimes through simplicity.

The passage beginning at figure 13 (m. 76) is unpredictable, even though it is based on a series of repeating eighth-note chords. Stravinsky strips the music of all harmonic and melodic variety. The orchestra, in effect, functions as a kind of giant, polychordal drum, repeating the same chord 32 times in succession (see Textbook, Example 20-6). By marking each iteration with a down bow, Stravinsky eliminates the slight alternation of strong and weak that is often perceptible from standard back-and-forth (down-and-up) bowing, and by placing accents at irregular intervals, he eradicates any sense of a rhythmic pattern.

The polytonal harmony of this same passage posed further challenges to early listeners. Contrasting triads are juxtaposed simultaneously, with each of two instrumental groups—two sets of horns, high strings, low strings—playing its own chord in such a way that an E major chord sounds simultaneously with an E♭⁷ chord.

Violins, violas, horns 1–4: E♭⁷ chord (E♭-G-B♭-D♭)

Cellos, basses, horns 5–8: E major chord (F♭-A♭-C♭ = E-G♯-B)

At figure 14, Stravinsky juxtaposes arpeggiated chords in an even more jarring fashion: an implied B♭⁷ arpeggio in the English horn, against C major in the bassoons, against an alternation of E major and E minor in the cellos (see Example 20-7 in the Textbook). Each chord is perfectly tonal within itself, but the simultaneous sounding of these chords rubbed many ears the wrong way, at least on first hearing in 1913. Within a decade, however, the elemental power of the score had won over a large following of critics and listeners alike.

156 Mikrokosmos, Book 6, No. 148:
Six Dances in Bulgarian Rhythm, No. 1
(between 1932 and 1939)
Bartók

1:08.69

In his own compositions, Bartók often incorporated the kind of irregular meters that characterize a good deal of the folk music of eastern Europe. The first of his *Six Dances in Bulgarian Rhythm* from his *Mikrokosmos,* Book 6, is built on a metrical pattern notated as:

$$\frac{4+2+3}{8}$$

This kind of meter is sometimes referred to as complex meter, and although it ostensibly had its origins in folk music, it found its way into much modernist music as well. The simultaneous contrast of tonal centers is also notable here. In m. 4–12, for example, Bartók contrasts a rising seven-note motif outlining an E major scale in the left hand with a downward melodic idea that corresponds to a Phrygian scale (in keyboard terms, a downward scale from E on the white notes, without an F♯).

157   Piano Sonata No. 7, op. 83 (1939–1942)
Third movement: Allegro precipitato
Sergei Prokofiev (1891–1953)

CD13, Track 11
Book p. 534

0:46.88

1:29

2:17.54

Radical primitivism in music was expressed by composers who wrote pieces emphasizing motoric rhythm: speed, extreme dynamics, repetitive patterns, and dissonant harmony. Prokofiev, an excellent pianist who toured throughout Europe and the United States before World War II, wrote numerous sonatas, concertos, and collections of pieces for his instrument. The Toccata, opus 11 (1912), is based on a symmetrical structure surrounding the tonic (D minor), to which the music returns constantly. A more intricate and satisfying work of this type is the finale of his Piano Sonata no. 7 in B♭ Major. Prokofiev labels this movement *precipitato*, and the performer has to play at a sufficient tempo to achieve the desired effect. As the cascading octaves and chords leap chromatically around the keyboard, a three-note bass figure in octaves (B♭-D♭-B♭) anchors the piece. One may ask: Is Prokofiev parodying (or honoring) a popular musical style he would have heard during his years in the West? Or is the figure intended to be objective, the result of pure composition, so that the listener should discount her or his assumptions (if there are any)? Either approach can produce different results, and both are valid, even if one decides that one is more satisfying.

158 Saudades do Brasil (1921)
Darius Milhaud (1892–1974)

158a No. 5, "Ipanema"

CD13, Track 12

Book p. 536

158b No. 6, "Gavea"

Composers can and often do adapt the music of cultures not their own. The French composer Darius Milhaud (1892–1974) drew on Latin American tunes and dance rhythms in his *Saudades do Brasil* ("Nostalgia for Brazil"). These dances integrate popular dance rhythms into a harmonic idiom that is delightfully unpredictable. Milhaud's ample use of polytonality distinguishes his music from the sounds one would have actually heard in the streets of, say, Rio de Janeiro; yet the rhythms are true-to-life enough to provide the music with a decidedly Brazilian flavor.

159 The Banshee (1925)
Henry Cowell (1897–1965)

CD13, Track 14
Book p. 538

Explanation of Symbols

"The Banshee" is played on the open strings of the piano, the player standing at the crook. Another person must sit at the keyboard and hold down the damper pedal throughout the composition. The whole work should be played an octave lower than written.

R. H. stands for "right hand." L. H. stands for "left hand." Different ways of playing the strings are indicated by a letter over each tone, as follows:

(A) indicates a sweep with the flesh of the finger from the lowest string up to the note given.

(B) sweep lengthwise along the string of the note given with flesh of finger.

(C) sweep up and back from lowest A to highest B-flat given in this composition.

(D) pluck string with flesh of finger, where written, instead of octave lower.

(E) sweep along three notes together, in the same manner as (B).

(F) sweep in the manner of (B) but with the back of finger-nail instead of flesh.

(G) when the finger is half way along the string in the manner of (F), start a sweep along the same string with the flesh of the other finger, thus partly damping the sound.

(H) sweep back and forth in the manner of (C), but start at the same time from both above and below, crossing the sweep in the middle.

(I) sweep along five notes, in the manner of (B).

(J) same as (I) but with back of finger-nails instead of flesh of finger.

(K) sweep along in manner of (J) with nails of both hands together, taking in all notes between the two outer limits given.

(L) sweep in manner of (C) with flat of hand instead of single finger.

Although the 20th century brought relatively few technical changes to the piano itself, composers developed many novel ways of using the existing instrument. In *The Banshee,* the Californian composer Henry Cowell calls on the performer to manipulate directly by hand the strings inside the instrument. *The Banshee* actually requires two performers, although the only responsibility of the one at the keyboard is to keep the damper pedal down throughout the entire work. The other player stands in the crook of the instrument and touches the strings with his or her fingers. Cowell's explanation of the special performance symbols for the work takes up almost as much space as the score itself. The opening of the piece calls for the standing player to "sweep with the flesh of the finger from the lowest string up to the note given," ending with another lengthwise sweep of the finger on the string of that highest note. Different sounds are gradually introduced: the sweep concludes with a pluck of strings, then with a sweep along the strings of three notes together, then sweeping with the back of the fingernails instead of the fleshy part of the finger, and so on.

At the time of composition in 1925, the unearthly effect was unlike anything anyone had heard before that time. The eerie quality of the sound fits with the work's title. In Cowell's own words, a banshee is "a woman of the Inner World . . . who is charged with the duty of taking your soul into the Inner World when you die . . . She has to come to the outer plane for this purpose, and she finds the outer plane very uncomfortable and unpleasant, so you will hear her wailing at the time of a death in your family."

160 **Pierrot lunaire** (1912)
Arnold Schoenberg (1874–1951)

160a No. 7, "Der kranke Mond" ("The Sick Moon")

CD13, Track 15
Book p. 545

Du nächtig todeskranker Mond
Dort auf des Himmels schwarzem Pfühl,
Dein Blick, so fiebernd übergroß,
Bannt mich wie fremde Melodie

An unstillbarem Liebesleid
Stirbst du, an Sehnsucht, tief erstickt,
Du nächtig todeskranker Mond
Dort auf des Himmels schwarzem Pfühl.

Den Liebsten, der im Sinnenrausch
Gedankenlos zur Liebsten schleicht,
Belustigt deiner Strahlen Spiel—
Dein bleiches, qualgebornes Blut,

Du nächtig todeskranker Mond.

You dark moon, deathly ill,
Laid over heaven's sable pillow,
Your fever-swollen gaze
Enchants me like alien melody.

You die of insatiable pangs of love,
Suffocated in longing,
You dark moon, deathly ill,
Laid over heaven's sable pillow.

The hotblooded lover
Slinking heedless to the tryst
You hearten with your play of light,
Your pale blood wrung from torment,

You dark moon, deathly ill.

Heilge Kreuze sind die Verse,
Dran die Dichter stumm verbluten,
Blindgeschlagen von der Geier
Flatterndem Gespensterschwarme!

In den Leibern schwelgten Schwerter,
Prunkend in des Blutes Scharlach!

Heilge Kreuze sind die Verse,
Dran die Dichter stumm verbluten.

Tot das Haupt—erstarrt die Locken—
Fern, verweht der Lärm des Pöbels.
Langsam sinkt die Sonne nieder,
Eine rote Königskrone.—
Heilge Kreuze sind die Verse!

Poems are poets' holy crosses
On which they bleed in silence,
Struck blind by phantom swarms
Of fluttering vultures.

Swords have feasted on their bodies,
Reveling in the scarlet blood!

Poems are poets' holy crosses
On which they bleed in silence.

Dead the head, the tresses stiffened,
Far away the noisy rabble.
Slowly the sun sinks,
A red royal crown.—
Poems are poets' holy crosses.

160c No. 21, "O alter Duft" ("O redolence of Old")

CD13, Track 17
Book p. 545

No. 160 Schoenberg: *Pierrot lunaire*   ■   **449**

O alter Duft aus Märchenzeit,
Berauschest wieder meine Sinne;
Ein närrisch Heer von Schelmerein
Durchschwirrt die leichte Luft.

Ein glückhaft Wünschen macht mich froh
Nach Freuden, die ich lang verachtet:
O alter Duft aus Märchenzeit,
Berauschest wieder mich!

All meinen Unmut gab ich preis;
Aus meinem sonnumrahmten Fenster
Beschau ich frei die liebe Welt

Und träum hinaus in selge Weiten . . .
O alter Duft—aus Märchenzeit!

O redolence from fairytale times,
Bewitch again my senses!
A knavish swarm of silly pranks
Buzzes down the gentle breeze.

A happy impulse calls me back
To joys I have long neglected:
O redolence from fairytale times,
Bewitch me again!

All my ill humors I've renounced;
From my sun-framed window
I behold untrammeled the beloved world

And dream me out to blissful vistas . . .
O redolence from fairytale times.

Pierrot is one of the stock masked characters from the Italian *commedia dell'arte,* a melancholy, moon-struck clown who lives in a state of constant longing. The poetic cycle *Pierre lunaire* by the Belgian poet Albert Giraud (1860–1929) draws on the mask as a metaphor for the human manners that conceal deeper emotions, and Schoenberg was deeply attracted to this imagery. The atonality of No. 7 ("The Sick Moon") makes the moon seem far more ill than any tonal idiom could. Schoenberg projects the violence of the text in No. 14 ("The Cross") by having the voice make leaps of ninths, diminished and augmented octaves, and other nontriadic intervals, thereby undermining any sense of a tonal center. The final work in Schoenberg's setting of 21 songs from this cycle is particularly haunting for the way in which it conjures up the specter of tonality. The text speaks of a longing for the old "fairy tale times," yet the poetic persona is fully aware that such times will never return, if indeed they existed at all. Schoenberg's music fits the text perfectly: in the opening piano passage, the "walking" bass and the triads in the upper voices sound almost like a chorale by J. S. Bach, but the harmonic distortions are more than enough to create a distorted, grotesque image of the musical past. The voice ends in a barely audible whisper in a barely audible range.

Sprechstimme, the style of singing called for throughout *Pierrot lunaire,* reinforces the surreal quality of the text and music. *Sprechstimme* (literally, "speech-voice," with "voice" understood here in the sense of "singing") is neither speech nor song, but a means of declamation somewhere between the two. Unlike speech, in *Sprechstimme* the vocalist must articulate specified pitches and rhythms. Instead of sustaining a pitch as in the conventional method of singing, however, the performer allows the pitch to drop rather in the same way one's voice drops with the enunciation of a spoken word. *Sprechstimme* is indicated by means of standard notes with a small *x* through the stem. The effect is unique: as song, it falls short of lyricism, and intentionally so, while as speech, it constitutes a purposefully exaggerated, overblown kind of delivery. It occupies a kind of twilight zone between speech and song that calls attention to the essentially artificial distinction between the two.

161 Five Pieces for String Quartet,
Op. 5, No. 4 (1908)
Anton Webern (1883–1945)

CD13, Track 18

Book p. 547

Anton Webern's *Five Pieces for String Quartet,* Op. 5 (1908) is a series of miniatures that concentrates its resources into a remarkably intense form of expression. Like most atonal works, the fourth of these five pieces uses a limited number of building blocks—in this case, groups of four or five notes—sometimes fewer, sometimes more, but rarely very many more. These units tend to avoid triads, both in their linear (melodic) and vertical (harmonic) alignments. Webern, like Schoenberg and Berg, saw himself as a traditionalist who continued in the tradition of Beethoven and Brahms by manipulating motivic ideas in a process that Schoenberg called "developing variation." The extreme brevity of the movements in Webern's Op. 5, the absence of a tonal center, and the consistent avoidance of strong cadences and any long-range sense of meter all make it difficult to hear this process of development, at least on first listening.

Fortunately, set theory, which was developed in the third quarter of the 20th century by the American scholar Allen Forte, among others, provides us with a framework for identifying the constituent elements that go into most atonal music. Forte proposed a system for identifying and clarifying the relationship of the relatively small units ("cells" or "sets") that together provide the building blocks for a typical atonal composition. These sets can consist of anywhere between two and ten pitch-classes. A pitch-class is any manifestation of a particular pitch, regardless of register; thus the pitch-class A-F can be used for units that go either down a major third or up a minor sixth—or down a tenth, and so on. There is a finite number of set types—220 to be exact—that can be created out of all the various combinations of pitch-classes (see Textbook, Focus, p. 550).

In analysis, these combinations of differing size are identified by a series of numbers reflecting the prime form of the set, beginning with 0 (the lowest note of the set) and moving upward by half-step. Thus the tetrachord set C-D♯-F-G would be called 0-3-5-7 because D♯ is three half-steps above C (0), F is 5 half-steps above C, and G is seven half-steps above C. Sets can be presented either simultaneously (as a "chord") or successively (as a "melody").

Looking at the score of Webern's Op. 5, No. 4, we can see that two sets play an important role in the opening measures. Set A (0-1-5-6 = B-C-E-F) is presented in the two upper voices in m. 1; set B (0-1-6-7 = B-C-F-F♯) at the beginning of m. 2. The pitches of set A recur on the final half-beat of m. 2; set B appears as a melodic line in the first violin in m. 3–4, then again in the second violin (m. 4) transposed down a fifth. Identifying pitch-class sets can be a hit-or-miss process at times: some sets occur only once or twice in a piece and cannot really be considered to have structural importance. The identification of sets can nevertheless be extremely helpful for making audibly coherent a work of music that might otherwise seem shapeless.

162 Wozzeck, Act I, Scene I (1925)
Alban Berg (1885–1935)

CD14, Track 1
Book p. 547

Note: This edition is a piano-vocal reduction of Berg's original score for voices and orchestra.

1:14.16

2:56.21

3:58.38

5:36.42

7:24.27

*) ♩=30 bis ♩=42-48 (entspricht <u>dann</u> dem Viertel des folgenden ¾ Takts [201])

1. AKT
1. SZENE

Zimmer des Hauptmanns (Frühmorgens). Hauptmann auf einem Stuhl vor einem Spiegel. Wozzeck rasiert den Hauptmann.

HAUPTMANN: Langsam, Wozzeck, langsam! Eins nach dem Andern! *(unwillig)* Er macht mir ganz schwindlich . . . *(bedeckt Stirn und Augen mit der Hand—wieder beruhigt. Wozzeck unterbricht seine Arbeit)*

HAUPTMANN: Was soll ich denn mit den zehn Minuten anfangen, die Er heut' zu früh fertig wird? *(energischer)* Wozzeck, bedenk' Er, Er hat noch seine schönen dreißig Jahr' zu leben! Dreißig Jahre: macht dreihundert und sechzig Monate und erst wie viel Tage, Stunden, Minuten! Was will Er denn mit der ungeheuren Zeit all' anfangen? *(wieder streng)* Teil' Er sich ein, Wozzeck!

WOZZECK: Jawohl, Herr Hauptmann!

HAUPTMANN: *(geheimnisvoll)* Es wird mir ganz angst um die Welt, wenn ich an die Ewigkeit denk'. "Ewig," das ist ewig! (das sieht Er ein.) Nun ist es aber wieder nicht ewig, sondern ein Augenblick, ja, ein Augenblick! Wozzeck, es schaudert mich, wenn ich denke, daß sich die Welt in einem Tag herumdreht: drum kann ich auch kein Mühlrad mehr sehn, oder ich werde melancholisch!

WOZZECK: Jawohl, Herr Hauptmann!

HAUPTMANN: Wozzeck, Er sieht immer so verhetzt aus! Ein guter Mensch tut das nicht. Ein guter Mensch, der sein gutes Gewissen hat, tut alles langsam . . . Red' Er doch was, Wozzeck. Was ist heut für ein Wetter?

WOZZECK: Sehr schlimm, Herr Hauptmann! Wind!

HAUPTMANN: Ich spür's schon, 's ist so was Geschwindes draußen; so ein Wind macht mir den Effekt, wie eine Maus. *(pfiffig)* Ich glaub; wir haben so was aus Südnord?

ACT ONE
SCENE ONE

(The Captain's room. Early morning. The Captain is sitting on a chair in front of a mirror, while Wozzeck is shaving him.)

CAPTAIN: Easy, Wozzeck, easy! Do take your time, man! *(anxiously)* You make me quite giddy. *(Covers his forehead and eyes with his hand. Wozzeck stops what he is doing. The Captain steadies himself)*

CAPTAIN: What shall I do with the time you save in ten minutes, if you finish early today? *(more vigorously)* Wozzeck, consider, you surely still have almost thirty years to live yet . . . Thirty years . . . that's three hundred and sixty months to go . . . and how many days and hours and minutes! . . . What will you do with the great expanse of time before you now? *(serious again)* Make up your mind, Wozzeck!

WOZZECK: Yes sir, I will sir.

CAPTAIN: *(mysteriously)* It makes me afraid for the world to think of eternity. Always—that's "eternal" . . . (you understand). But then again, it cannot be always . . . but a mere moment, yes, a moment. Wozzeck, I'm terrified when I'm thinking that the whole world in one short day revolves. And if I see a mill-wheel that turns, it always gives me melancholia.

WOZZECK: Yes sir, I see sir.

CAPTAIN: Wozzeck, your face always looks so harrassed. A worthy man takes his time, a worthy man with a conscience that's undefiled does all things slowly. *Do* say something, Wozzeck. Come tell me, how's the weather?

WOZZECK: Not good. Not good, sir. Wind . . .

CAPTAIN: I feel it . . . there's something so swift outside there. Such a wind always seems to me just like a mouse. *(artfully)* I think there's something blowing from South-North . . .

Berg tended to take a more liberal approach to serial composition than either Schoenberg or Webern. The first movement of his *Lyric Suite* for string quartet uses three different (yet related) rows, and not all of its six movements are serial: only the outer movements are entirely dodecaphonic. The third movement is serial in its outer sections but not in its trio, and only the trios of the fifth movement are written in the twelve-tone method. Berg manipulates the basic row of the work (See Textbook, Example 21-6a) in ingenious ways. By rotating one derivation of the row—that is, by beginning it on a pitch other than 0, Berg is able to create a derivative row with the succession of pitches A-B♭-B-F. These pitches hold a symbolic meaning for Berg: keeping in mind that in German, "B" is called "H" and "B♭" is called simply "B," these pitches represent the composer's own initials (A-B) and those of his secret lover, Hanna Fuchs (H-F). Berg calls special attention to this tetrachord—this group of four notes—at the beginning of the movement, where every voice plays some version of this grouping:

- First violin: P-0 (beginning on 0). The first full statement of P-0 occurs in m. 2–3.
- Second violin: P-7 (rotated, beginning on 9). The first full statement of P-7 occurs in m. 3–4.
- Viola: P-10 (rotated, beginning on 3). The first full statement of P-10 occurs in m. 3.

These three forms of the row, along with I-5, are the only ones Berg uses in this section. The *trio estatico* ("ecstatic trio") is freely composed, while the return of the opening section at m. 93 presents the opening section in a large-scale retrograde. The inverse relationship of opening and closing becomes especially clear when we compare the first and last few measures of the movement.

165 **Classical Symphony,** Op. 25, third
movement (1917)
Sergei Prokofiev (1891–1953)

CD14, Track 5
Book p. 564

III

Gavotta

0:37

1:05.64

The "Gavotta" from Prokofiev's *Classical Symphony* represents the artistic movement known as Neoclassicism. Prokofiev preserves the characteristic form and rhythms of the gavotte but transforms the melody and harmony in ways that are distinctively 20th-century. The movement is essentially in D major, yet the harmony consistently avoids any strong cadence in this key. When a cadence in the tonic finally arrives at the end of the second reprise, there is a strong sense of rhythmic arrival, but the harmony has been so skewed as to make the tonic sound unexpected at this point. The section that follows provides the thematic and textural contrast one would expect in the trio of such a dance: the droning open fifths evoke the sound of a bagpipe, hurdy-gurdy, or other similar folk instrument. And when the opening reprise returns in m. 29, it is now reorchestrated, with the winds taking the lead. The piece ends not with a bang but a whimper: pianissimo, understated, tongue in cheek. Neoclassical composers prided themselves on avoiding emotional extremes, bombast, and monumentality.

166 Aufstieg und Fall der Stadt Mahagonny:
"Alabama Song" (1927)
Kurt Weill (1900–1950)

CD14, Track 6
Book p. 566

Aus der geschlossenen Gardine treten mit einem großen Koffer Jenny und die 6 Mädchen, setzen sich auf den Koffer und singen den Alabama-Song.

Note: This edition is a piano-vocal reduction of Weill's original score for voices and orchestra.

0:31.9

No. 166 Weill: *Aufstieg und Fall der Stadt Mahagonny*　■　**483**

Kurt Weill and the poet Bertolt Brecht (1898–1956) collaborated on a series of stage productions in the 1920s and 1930s that emphasized a sense of aesthetic distance between the artist and his work and the audience and the work. Speaking in the third person (a verbal technique of distancing), the composer announced that "Brecht and Weill have investigated the question of music's role in the theater. They have concluded that music cannot further the action of a play or create its background. Instead, it achieves its proper value when it interrupts the action at the right moments."

Weill's second collaboration with Brecht was *Aufstieg und Fall der Stadt Mahagonny* ("Rise and Fall of the City of Mahagonny," 1928–29), a satire on capitalism that takes place in a fictional city (Mahagonny) in which the only crime is poverty. Everything is legal as long as it can be paid for. The "Alabama Song," sung by Jenny (a prostitute) and her six cohorts, assumes the outward form of a traditional aria, with a declamatory introduction and a soaring conclusion, but the words are surreal ("Oh! Moon of Alabama we now must say goodbye, / We've lost our good old mama and must have whisky oh you know why.") and, oddly enough for an opera otherwise in German, the text of this number is in English. All this creates a sense of distance—objectivity—that is magnified by the discordant sound of the honky-tonk-style accompaniment.

Performance note: The soloist heard in this recording, Lotte Lenya (1898–1981) was married to the composer Kurt Weill. She sang leading roles in the original productions of several of her husband's works, including *Die Dreigroschenoper* ("The Threepenny Opera"). The studio recording here was made in New York City in the 1950s. Lenya also appeared in several films late in her life, including the James Bond film *From Russia With Love* (1963), in which she played the evil Rosa Klebb.

167 Music for Strings, Percussion, and Celesta, third movement (1936)

Bartók

CD14, Track 7

Book p. 567

2:26.31

*) *Griffbezeichnung* / indique la manière de toucher

3:43.85

490 Bartók: *Music for Strings, Percussion, and Celesta*

5:39.94

No. 167 Bartók: *Music for Strings, Percussion, and Celesta*   ■   **497**

Béla Bartók's *Music for Strings, Percussion, and Celesta* (1936) is written for an unusual combination of instruments: a double string orchestra (including harp), celesta (a keyboard instrument that mimics the sound of small bells), and a battery of percussion instruments (timpani, piano, xylophone, bass drum, side drum, cymbals, tam-tam). The work is tightly integrated, with all four movements deriving their principal thematic ideas from the fugue subject of the opening movement.

The third movement of *Music for Strings, Percussion, and Celesta* is full of unusual sonorities. It opens with an extended solo on a single note in the upper reaches of the xylophone—a note so high, in fact, that its pitch (F) can scarcely be perceived as a pitch at all. The xylophone is soon joined by a timpani playing glissandos. The movement as a whole is structured around the principle of a symmetrical or arch form, by which the music progresses toward a mid-point and then more or less retraces its steps. This particular movement centers on m. 49–50, which present an essentially retrograde form of m. 47–48. The music "turns" upon this moment. On the whole, the movement can be broken down as follows:

A	B	C	D	E	D	C	B	A
Measure	1	6	20	35	45	65	74	77	80

The proportions are not strict—Bartók was seldom pedantic about such matters—but the overall impression is one of growth, development, climax, and return to an original state. A glance at the opening and closing measures shows the gradual addition of instruments: xylophone, then timpani and cello. The movement ends with instruments dropping out: first the violas, then the xylophone, ending with the timpani. The idea of symmetry operates at various points throughout this movement on a smaller scale as well. The opening rhythm of the xylophone gesture, for example, is symmetrical in its own right, with its midpoint at the downbeat of m. 3.

168 **Alexander Nevsky,** Op. 78, No. 4: "Vstavaite, ludi russkie" ("Arise, People of Russia") (1938)
Prokofiev

CD14, Track 8
Book p. 569

8 Вставайте, люди русские 4. Arise, Ye Russian People

1:40

No. 168 Prokofiev: *Alexander Nevsky* ∎ **507**

The film *Alexander Nevsky,* directed by Sergei Eisenstein, is based on the true story of Grand Duke Alexander of Novgorod, who defeated the Swedes on the River Neva (hence "Nevsky" in his popular name) in the year 1240 and went on to repel an army of Teutonic knights in 1242 in a battle that took place on the frozen surface of Lake Chudskoye. In the film's climactic scene, the ice breaks and swallows the invaders. In 1939, Prokofiev turned his brilliant score for this movie into a cantata for mezzo-soprano, chorus, and large orchestra. The rousing fourth movement of this work ("Arise, People of Russia") like much of the rest of the score, integrates folksong-like melodies (of Prokofiev's own invention) with a harmonic idiom that is essentially triadic. The occasional modal and chromatic inflections are extremely limited, for this was music written to appeal to mass audiences and their spirit of patriotism. This kind of writing was actively promoted by Soviet authorities under the banner of what they called socialist realism, a readily accessible style that evokes the music of the people in an overwhelmingly optimistic tone (see Textbook, Primary Evidence: Socialist Realism).

The Soviet government was quick to recognize the potential of film and film music to galvanize patriotic fervor. The state itself financed Eisenstein's *Alexander Nevsky* in the late 1930s at a time when German invasion appeared imminent: the film's plot is deeply nationalistic and transparently anti-German. Soldiers of the Red Army were actually used as extras in the movie. But after signing the Non-Aggression Pact with Hitler in 1939 (the same agreement whose secret annex also spelled out the later dismemberment of Poland by both Germany and the Soviet Union), Stalin had the film removed from circulation, only to have it rushed back into theaters after Germany's surprise invasion of the Soviet Union in June of 1941. The film's powerful images were made all the more evocative by Prokofiev's stirring score.

169a Bonaparte's Retreat (traditional)
(recorded 1937)
William H. Stepp (1875–1947)

CD14, Track 9
Book p. 572

While collecting folksongs and fiddle tunes in eastern Kentucky in 1937, the folklorists Alan and John Lomax recorded several numbers by "Fiddler Bill" Stepp, including one variously known as "Bonaparte's Retreat" or simply "Bonypart." The performance (reproduced here) was later transcribed by Ruth Crawford Seeger and included in *Our Singing Country,* an anthology of American folk music edited by the Lomaxes and published by Macmillan in 1941. It was from this source that Aaron Copland learned the tune that he would later incorporate into the "Hoe-down" from his *Rodeo* (II/169b).

CD14, Track 10
Book p. 572

HOE-DOWN
from
"RODEO"

AARON COPLAND

B. & H. 8896

B. & H. 8896

0:34.11

2:07.02

2:32.17

522 ■ No. 169b Copland: Hoe-down

Rodeo was Copland's second "American" ballet, commissioned and danced by Agnes de Mille and the Ballet Russe de Monte Carlo in 1942. Unlike its predecessor, *Billy the Kid, Rodeo's* scenario is quite lighthearted: a cowgirl wants to gain the attention of a champion wrangler but refuses to "dress like a girl"; when a more traditional rancher's daughter seems to be winning the young man's heart, the cowgirl shows up in a dress for the square dance finale, "Hoe-down," and wins the heart of the wrangler. (The discomfort of the cowgirl with traditional gender roles was said to be autobiographical for de Mille.)

De Mille, who choreographed the entire ballet before Copland had written single note of the music, specified several traditional tunes for the composer to include in the score. Copland went on to find Ruth Crawford Seeger's transcription of "Bonaparte's Retreat" in *Our Singing Country,* an anthology of American folk music edited by Alan and John Lomax and published in 1941. Copland makes the melody his own, thanks to colorful elements such as the "tuning up" at the beginning, the tension between conjunct and disjunct melodic lines, Stravinsky-like accents applied to the principal tune in the violins (which sound like "fiddles" in cross-tuning), and the beautiful depiction of a (temporary) technological breakdown at rehearsal 18.

170 Quatuor pour la fin du temps, first movement: "Liturgie de cristal" (1940)
Olivier Messiaen (1908–1992)

CD14, Track 11
Book p. 574

(*) *Glissando bref; id. aux passages similaires.*

Tous droits d'exécution réservés.
Copyright by DURAND & Cⁱᵉ 1942

The French composer Olivier Messiaen (1908–1992) wrote his *Quatuor pour la fin du temps* ("Quartet for the End of Time") while interred in a German prisoner-of-war camp in the early years of World War II. The only instruments at his disposal at the time were a clarinet, a violin, a cello, and a rickety piano. Although many inmates interpreted its title as an allusion to the end of their time in prison, the composer himself insisted that the true inspiration for the work came from Chapter 10 of the New Testament book of Revelation, in which an angel causes time to cease at the end of the world. Messiaen compared the opening movement, "Liturgy of Crystal" to "the harmonious silence of the firmament." The harmonics in the cello help create a particularly light, ethereal timbre: by touching the string lightly wherever a lozenge-shaped note is indicated, the cellist creates a pitch—a harmonic overtone—that actually sounds two octaves higher than the notated pitch.

But the "End of the Time" in the work's title is most directly evident in its organization of rhythm. The four voices operate on entirely different rhythmic levels: the violin and clarinet—which by the composer's own account reflect the songs of a nightingale and black-bird, respectively—are free, random, unpredictable. The cello and piano, in contrast, adhere to strict rhythmic and melodic patterns. The cello presents a fifteen-note melody eight and one-half times over the course of the movement (see Example 22-2 in Textbook).

The rhythmic pattern of the melody is palindromic—the same forward as backward—or as Messiaen himself called it, nonretrogradable. This is not obvious at first because the note values begin in the middle of the rhythmic sequence: time, after all, has been going on before the piece begins.

The piano's rhythm of seventeen note values, although not palindromic, is also repeated many times. As in the case of the cello, the rhythmic pattern begins and ends in the middle of two different measures and thus shifts constantly in relation to the bar line. Thematically, the piano repeats a sequence of 29 chords throughout, but the thematic and rhythmic patterns do not coincide. This structure resembles that of the medieval isorhythm (see Chapter 3), in which a melodic pattern (*color*) is played against an independent rhythmic pattern (*talea*). Although Messiaen himself was well aware of the technique of isorhythm, he maintained that his more immediate sources were the rhythmic structures of certain Hindu modes.

This movement also reminds us just how remote a work can be removed from the framework of triadic harmony. Although many of the piano's 29 chords (see Example 22-3 in Textbook) incorporate triadic harmonies, they also have multiple additional nonharmonic tones. The inner voices of chords 9 through 12, for example, present a series of first-inversion harmonies on G♭ major, G major, A♭ major, and A major, but the nonharmonic notes of the outer voices mask the sound of these triads. At the same time, the insistent F in the bass, which has been present since the very first chord, grounds the music around a semblance of a tonal center. Messiaen himself described the opening sonority as a "chord on the dominant"—in this case, of B♭ major, the tonality implied by the key signature—even though it does not function as such in the traditional sense.

171 **String Quartet No. 8,** third movement
(1960)

Dmitri Shostakovich (1906–1975)

CD14, Track 12
Book p. 575

0:40.28

527

1:34.98

2:03.90

2:52.53

The String Quartet No. 8 of the Russian composer Dmitri Shostakovich is heavily auto-biographical. "When I die," Shostakovich wrote to a friend, "it's hardly likely that someone will write a quartet dedicated to my memory. So I decided to write it myself." The work is saturated with a musical motif which the composer himself identified as his musical monogram: the notes D-E♭-C-B, which in the German system of notation (see p. 429) spell D-S (=Es =E♭)-C-H (=B♮), are shorthand for **D**mitri **Sch**ostakovich, the German transliteration of the composer's name. The piece as a whole is full of quotations from Shostakovich's operas, symphonies, and chamber works; it also includes snippets from Siegfried's funeral music in Wagner's *Götterdämmerung* and the first movement of Tchaikovsky's Sixth Symphony. The latter two are directly associated with the idea of death, as is the recurring *Dies irae* plainchant melody, the same tune used by Berlioz in the finale of his *Symphonie fantastique* (see Chapter 14).

Shostakovich dedicated his Eighth Quartet "to the memory of the victims of fascism and war"—that is, to the victims of the struggle against Nazi Germany in World War II—a sentiment wholly acceptable to Soviet authorities. But several of the composer's friends have since asserted that the work was Shostakovich's "suicide note," that the composer planned to swallow an overdose of sleeping pills after finishing this work, so depressed was he at having been forced to join the Communist Party. As is so often the case with Shostakovich, truth and fiction are difficult to separate. Eyewitness accounts of events in his life are not always reliable, many of them never having been committed to paper until after the composer's death. The music itself, however, clearly connects the images of Shostakovich (through the many quotations of his own music and of his musical monogram) and death (through the quotation of death-related music by other composers). In the final movement, the DSCH motif appears as a counterpoint to a quotation from the last scene of Shostakovich's opera *Lady Macbeth of the Mtsensk District* (1934), banned by the Soviet government, in which prisoners are being transported to Siberia. This could easily have been Shostakovich's own fate had he not agreed to join the Communist Party. Shostakovich used the ambiguity of the music as a shield for his own self-expression.

The third movement functions as a scherzo and assumes the form of a waltz, but it is a macabre kind of dance. The introduction begins with the DSCH theme in the first violin (D-E♭-C-H[B♮]), which soon (m. 20) reenters as the main motive, now jarringly discordant with the simple G minor accompaniment. Formally, the movement follows the standard scherzo-trio-scherzo pattern. It leads without a break into the finale.

CD14, Track 13
Book p. 579

Ain't Misbehavin'

Tune Ukulele
A D F♯ B
Capo on 1st Fret

Lyric by [13]
ANDY RAZAF

Music by
THOMAS WALLER and
HARRY BROOKS

Moderato

BOY__ Tho it's a fick-le age
GIRL__ Your type of man is rare,

With flirt-ing all the rage, Here is one bird with self-con-trol; Hap-py in-side my
I know you real-ly care, That's why my conscience never sleeps; When you're away some

cage. I know who I love best, Thumbs down for all the rest,
-where. Sure was a luck-y day, When fate sent you my way,

My love was giv-en, heart and soul; So it can stand the test.
And made you mine a-lone for keeps, Dit-to to all you say.

CHORUS
Slowly, with expression

No one to talk with, all by my-self, No one to walk with, but I'm happy on the shelf,

Ain't misbehav-in', I'm sav-in' my love for you._____ I know for certain

the one I love, I'm thru with flirtin', it's just you I'm think-in' of, Ain't mis-be-hav-in',

Ain't Misbehavin' - 3

0:56.4

532

I'm sav-in' my love for you. ___ Like Jack Horner in the cor-ner,

don't go no-where, what do I care, Your kiss-es are worth waitin' for, be - lieve me

I don't stay out late, don't care to go, I'm home a-bout eight, just me and my ra - di-o,

Ain't mis-be-havin' I'm sav-in' my love for you. you. ___

Ain't Misbehavin'- 3

You Will Love To Play This
NOVELTY PIANO SOLO
Flapperette
A Wonderful New Novelty
by JESSE GREER

Piano Score by
HAROLD POTTER

The most vital form of musical drama throughout the 20th century was the Broadway musical, a genre that took its name from the New York City street on or near which many prominent musical theaters are located. A direct descendant of the *Singspiel* or operetta—a play with songs—the Broadway musical is a commercial venture that requires considerable capital, but which can bring handsome returns to investors. Andrew Lloyd Webber's *Cats* ran for some 7,485 performances between 1982 and 2000; revivals of earlier musicals like Richard Rodgers's *Oklahoma!* and *South Pacific* and Jerome Kern's *Show Boat* testify to the continuing appeal of older repertory.

The plots of many early musicals were no more than a framework for a revue, in which a potpourri of acts followed in quick succession; song and dance were the dominant components of these shows. African Americans at the turn of the 20th century had began to produced musical comedies on Broadway that drew white audiences (and on occasion integrated casts). After a hiatus in the 1910s, the African-American musical genre was revived with *Shuffle Along* (1921, by Sissle and Blake, and including "I'm Just Wild about Harry"); *Blackbirds of 1928* (by Fields and McHugh, featuring "I Can't Give You Anything but Love"); and *Hot Chocolates* (1929), a collaboration between Andy Razaf, Harry Brooks, and Thomas "Fats" Waller, a brilliant songwriter, pianist, and entertainer who played an jazz-inflected style of ragtime known as "stride piano." *Hot Chocolates,* which started life as a Harlem nightclub revue, is now best known for the song "Ain't Misbehavin'," later the eponymous title of a successful Broadway revue of Waller songs in 1978.

Among the original cast of *Hot Chocolates* were the multitalented Cab Calloway and the trumpeter and bandleader Louis Armstrong (1901–1971). Although Calloway sang "Ain't Misbehavin'" in the show, Armstrong made his own recording with his "orchestra" (11 players) the same year the show opened. In Armstrong's version, the song (in the standard AABA song form) is played through three times; first as an ensemble, then sung by Armstrong in the improvisational style he was famous for, then as a platform for an skillful Armstrong solo. At one point he unexpectedly quotes a famous melody for humorous effect; this technique recalls similar references to the "Tristan chord" in works by Debussy and Berg previously discussed.

West Side Story: "Tonight" (Quintet) (1957)
Leonard Bernstein (1918–1990)

CD14, Track 14
Book p. 579

* If the scene is staged with more than the designated five people, the members of the gangs may sing with their respective leaders
(except in bars 103 - 125).

1:31.23

2:50.63

* The part of Anita may be augmented by voices in the wings from here to the end.

* The part of Maria may be augmented by voices in the wings from here to the end.

[Piano reduction of the original orchestral version]

Leonard Bernstein's *West Side Story* (1957) focuses on the problem of gang warfare between Puerto Ricans (The Sharks) and whites (The Jets) in New York City. The libretto, by Stephen Sondheim (who would go on to compose many hit musicals of his own), was unusually gritty and realistic by the standards of its time. It draws liberally on Shakespeare's *Romeo and Juliet,* featuring a pair of lovers from rival groups and ending in the death of one of them.

The Quintet "Tonight" is very much in the tradition of *Bella figlia del l'amore* from Verdi's *Rigoletto* (Anthology 2/138b). Dramatically, both revolve around the feeling of anticipation: the Sharks and Jets await their climactic conflict; the sultry Anita knows that she will get "her kicks" that night ("He'll walk in hot and tired. So what? Don't matter if he's tired, as long as he's hot"); and the two lovers, Tony and Maria, await their meeting ("Tonight, tonight won't be just any night."). The number builds gradually and becomes increasingly contrapuntal as it progresses, with a lyrical love duet between Tony and Maria that unfolds above the animosity of the rival choruses. Bernstein uses a jazz-like orchestration, a rapid alternation of duple and triple meters, and even *Sprechstimme* at one point to give the music a decidedly modern sound. But the overall shape of the movement—contrasting emotions expressed simultaneously— owes much to the traditions of 19th-century opera.

174 War Requiem: "Let us sleep now — Requiem aeternam — requiescat" (1962)
Benjamin Britten (1913–1976)

CD14, Track 15

Book p. 580

B. & H. 18940

2:36.73

Rather than simply setting the Latin text for the Requiem, Britten created a more telling context by adding several poems by Wilfred Owen (1893–1918), a soldier who led a rifle company in France and was killed just before the Armistice. Owen's remarkably modern and darkly ironic writing proved to be the perfect foil for the Latin text. To intensify the sense of postwar disorientation, Britten scored the work for three separate groups: a full orchestra with chorus and solo soprano, a chamber ensemble accompanying a solo tenor and bass, and a portative organ–led boys' choir. The three groups are separated spatially: in one performance, the orchestral group took center stage, the chamber ensemble stood on the right apron, and the boys' choir sang from the first tier, directly across from the other two groups and above and behind the audience, projecting an eerie, ill-defined sound.

The power of the *War Requiem* lies in the tripartite divide between the chorus and soprano (performing the traditional text in a modern reinterpretation of the oratorio), the boys' choir (also singing in Latin, but with a "traditional" church music sound in a concert hall setting), and the ensemble-accompanied male soloists, who intersperse the Owen material between the Latin; this has the effect of both universalizing and particularizing Owen's message. As the poet wrote in an unpublished preface to a collection he did not live to publish: "My subject is War, and the pity of War/The Poetry is in the pity . . . / All a poet can do today is warn" (Britten quoted this on the title page of his score).

The closing section, "Libera me," is interrupted by the final Owen setting ("It seemed that out of battle I escaped . . .") in which two soldiers meet "down some profound dull tunnel": "Strange friend," one addresses the other, "here is no cause to mourn." Toward the end of the poem, they realize "I am the enemy you killed, my friend." The two male soloists conclude with "Let us sleep now . . . ," sung to each other as a lullaby, while the chorus, boys' choir, organ, soprano soloist, and full orchestra gradually reenter for the first and only tutti in the entire oratorio ("In paradisum"). The effect is spellbinding, and the bells take up the F#/C♮ tritone with which the work began (and which has dominated much of the harmony throughout). The boys' choir ("Amen, amen") seems to resolve the dissonance to the open fifth F#/C#, but then the chord resolves to a F major triad, a surprising but highly effective close to one of the 20th century's great choral works.

Latin Text and Translation for Britten, War Requiem

In paridisum deducant te Angeli;
in tuo adventu suscipiant te Martyres,
et perducant te in civitatem sanctam Jerusalem.
Chorus Angelorum te suscipiat,
et cum Lazaro quondam paupere aeternam habeas requiem.

Requiem aeternam dona eis, Domine:
et lux perpetua luceat eis.
Requiescant in pace. Amen.

May angels lead you into Paradise;
May martyrs receive you at your coming,
and lead you into the holy city of Jerusalem.
May a choir of angels receive you,
and with Lazarus, once poor, may you have eternal rest.

Lord, grant them eternal rest,
and let perpetual light shine upon them.
Let them rest in peace. Amen.

175 Threnody for the Victims of Hiroshima (1960)
Krzysztof Penderecki (b. 1933)

CD14, Track 16
Book p. 583

SKRÓTY I SYMBOLE	ABBREVIATIONS AND SYMBOLS		SIGNES D'ABREVIATION ET SYMBOLES	ABKÜRZUNGEN UND SYMBOLE
ordinario	ordinario	ord.		
sul ponticello	sul ponticello	s. p.		
sul tasto	sul tasto	s. t.		
col legno	col legno	c. l.		
legno battuto	legno battuto	l. batt.		
podwyższenie o ¼ tonu	raised by ¼ tone	⸸	hausse la note d'un quart de ton	Erhöhung um ¼ Ton
podwyższenie o ¾ tonu	raised by ¾ tone	⸸	hausse la note de trois quarts de ton	Erhöhung um ¾ Ton
obniżenie o ¼ tonu	lowered by ¼ tone	♭	abaisse la note d'un quart de ton	Erniedrigung um ¼ Ton
obniżenie o ¾ tonu	lowered by ¾ tone	d	abaisse la note de trois quarts de ton	Erniedrigung um ¾ Ton
najwyższy dźwięk instrumentu (wysokość nieokreślona)	highest note of the instrument (indefinite pitch)	▲	le son le plus aigu de l'instrument (hauteur indéterminée)	höchster Ton des Instrumentes (unbestimmte Tonhöhe)
grać między podstawkiem i strunnikiem	play between bridge and tailpiece		jouer entre le chevalet et le cordier	zwischen Steg und Saitenhalter spielen
arpeggio na 4 strunach za podstawkiem	arpeggio on 4 strings behind the bridge		arpège sur 4 cordes entre le chevalet et le cordier	Arpeggio zwischen Steg und Saitenhalter (4 Saiten)
grać na strunniku (arco)	play on tailpiece (arco)		jouer sur le cordier (arco)	auf dem Saitenhalter spielen (arco)
grać na podstawku	play on bridge		jouer sur le chevalet	auf dem Steg spielen
efekt perkusyjny: uderzać w górną płytę skrzypiec żabka lub czubkami palców	percussion effect: strike the upper sounding board of the violin with the nut or the finger-tips		effet de percussion: frapper la table de dessus du violon avec le talon de l'archet ou avec les bouts des doigt	Schlagzeugeffekt: mit dem Frosch oder mit Fingerspitze die Decke schlagen
kilka nieregularnych zmian smyczka	several irregular changes of bow	⊓ V	plusieurs changements d'archet irréguliers	mehrere unregelmäßige Bogenwechsel
molto vibrato	molto vibrato	∿∿∿∿	molto vibrato	molto vibrato
bardzo wolne vibrato w obrębie ćwierćtonu, uzyskane przez przesuwanie palca	very slow vibrato with a ¼ tone frequency difference produced by sliding the finger	∿∿∿	vibrato très lent à interval d'un quart de ton par le déplacement du doigt	sehr langsames Vibrato mit ¼ - Ton-Frequenzdifferenz durch Fingerverschiebung
bardzo szybkie i nierytmizowane tremolo	very rapid not rhythmicized tremolo	⪪	trémolo très rapide, mais sans rythme précis	sehr schnelles, nicht rhytmisiertes Tremolo

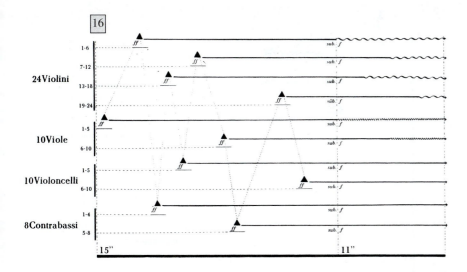

24Violini
1-6
7-12
13-18
19-24

10Viole
1-5
6-10

10Violoncelli
1-5
6-10

8Contrabassi
1-4
5-8

15"   11"

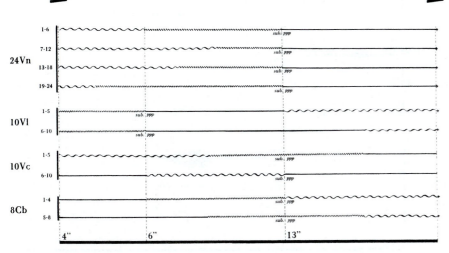

24Vn
1-6
7-12
13-18
19-24

10Vl
1-5
6-10

10Vc
1-5
6-10

8Cb
1-4
5-8

4"   6"   13"

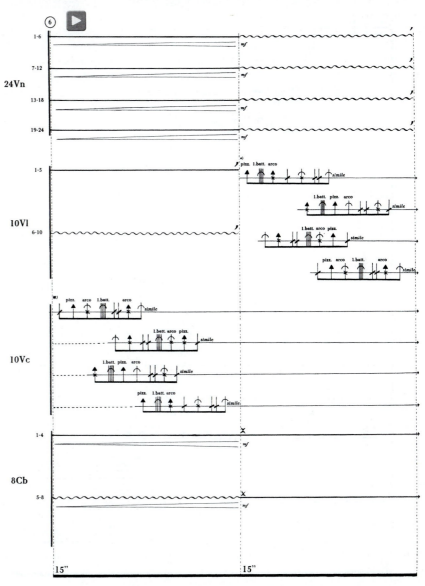

24Vn
1-6
7-12
13-18
19-24

10Vl
1-5
6-10

10Vc

8Cb
5-8

15"   15"

*) Każdy instrumentalista wybiera sobie jedno z 4 podanych ugrupowań i realizuje je (w wyznaczonym odcinku czasu) tak szybko, jak tylko można.
Jeder Instrumentalist wählt eine der angegebenen 4 Gruppierungen und spielt sie (im bestimmten Zeitabschnitt) so schnell wie möglich.
Each instrumentalist chooses one of the 4 given groups and executes it (within a fixed space of time) as rapidly as possible.
le exécutant choisit un des 4 groupements donnés et l'exécute (dans le segment de temps indiqué) aussi vite que possible.

1:25.14

No. 175 Penderecki: *Threnody for the Victims of Hiroshima*   ■   551

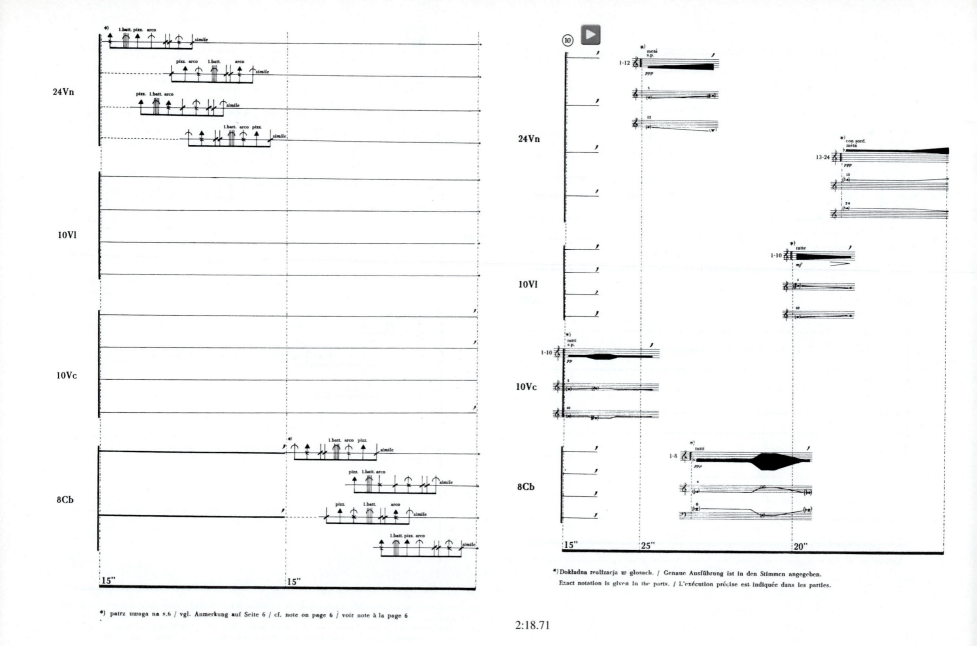

*) Dokładna realizacja w głosach. / Genaue Ausführung ist in den Stimmen angegeben.
Exact notation is given in the parts. / L'exécution précise est indiquée dans les parties.

2:18.71

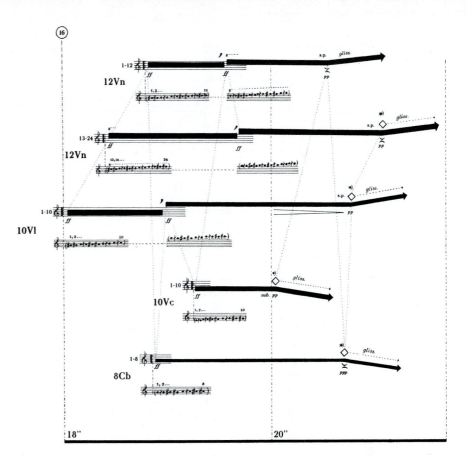

*) flażoletu kwartowe / Flageolettöne / flageolet tones / harmoniques

* patrz uwaga na s. 8 / vgl. Anmerkung auf Seite 8 / cf note on page 8   voir note à la page 8

6:40

7:46

No. 175 Penderecki: *Threnody for the Victims of Hiroshima*   ■   **557**

In this work (originally titled *8'37"*), the Polish composer Penderecki calls for a unique combination of sounds from an orchestra consisting of 52 *obbligato* stringed instruments (24 violins, 10 violas, 10 cellos, 8 double basses). Conventional sonorities and textures are dispensed with. At times the string players are asked to create sharp, percussive sounds by snapping strings against the fingerboard. At other times they must produce a different kind of percussive sound by striking the body of the instrument with the fingertips. Penderecki's score grants considerable freedom to the performers at many points. He asks individual players at several points to play simply "the highest note possible." At other points, he directs different groups of instruments to play with vibrato at different rates of speed, indicated only generally by the size of the wavy line in the score; the precise speed is left up to individual players. On still other occasions, individual performers are free to choose from a group of four different notational sequences and to perform the chosen group "as rapidly as possible." The work features no meter and no bar lines: durations are indicated by timings that run underneath the bottom of each system of the score.

Other elements of the score, however, are extremely precise. Penderecki uses microtones —intervals smaller than a half-step in the diatonic scale—at many points in the score. Western musicians had long been aware of microtones, but principally as a theoretical idea. It was not until the 20th century that composers like Ives, Bartók, Berg, Copland, and Ligeti began to use microtones in their works. Penderecki's *Threnody* explores these possibilities to an unprecedented degree, concluding with a massive quarter-tone cluster of tones and microtones spanning two octaves and played by all 52 instruments.

The form of Penderecki's *Threnody* offers a comparable mixture of precision and imprecision. It is structured around sonorities, dynamics, and textures rather than themes or key areas. Although it resists any ready-made formal category, its ever-changing surface suggests a division into five large sections:

1. m. 1–5   High register, varying vibrato
2. m. 6–9   Pizzicato and bowed passages played on the tailpiece
3. m. 10–25   Expanding and contracting tone clusters
4. m. 26–62   Percussive, pointilistic sounds, with much tremolo
5. m. 63–end   Gradual return of tone clusters

After he heard the first performances of the work, Penderecki felt that, despite the abstract origins of its composition, the piece had proved emotionally powerful in realization. He decided to dedicate the work to the victims of Hiroshima. In 1964, he wrote, "Let the *Threnody* express my firm belief that the sacrifice of Hiroshima will never be forgotten and lost." He was by no means the first to change his mind about a work's title (recall the dedication to Napoleon on the title page of Beethoven's Symphony no. 3 in Chapter 15).

176 String Quartet 1931: IV. Finale
Ruth Crawford (1901–1953)

CD15, Track 1

Book p. 585

114-40013-45

559

114-40013-45

114-40013-45

1:00.57

114-40013-45

The *String Quartet 1931* in four continuous movements displays the features specifically associated with Charles Seeger's theories, yet exhibits Ruth Crawford's more personal compositional traits: simultaneous parts at different "speeds," alternation between stepwise and displaced passages, extreme textures (for example, one solo line supported by three trills or held notes), sustained overlapping dissonances, close canonic writing, and the lack of vertically displayed chords amid a primarily contrapuntal texture.

Anticipating Bartók's procedure in the third movement of *Music for Strings, Percussion, and Celesta*, Crawford structures the finale (*Allegro possibile*) as a quasi-palindrome in a dialogue between the first violin (which Crawford calls "Voice 1") and the rest of the quartet ("Voice 2"). Crawford uses a ten-note row, and employs rotation (in which the prime form of the row simply "picks up" somewhere after its first note, without transposition) every 20 measures or so. As Voice 1 continues, it slowly accumulates additional notes in its phrases, while the answering octave phrases in Voice 2 remove notes at the same rate. In measure 58, the four parts reach the midpoint, hold the chord (a "consonant" C first-inversion chord), then begin the process of "dissonation" by playing through the preceding music in reverse a half-step higher, until the opening texture is restored, closing with the same three fortissimo notes in Voice 1 (a half-step higher). Even if the pitch content is (intentionally) dissociative and difficult to hear palindromically, the overall arch of the rhythm is clearly audible, even with its ever-changing surface; compare Crawford's approach with Messiaen's nonretrogradable rhythm in his *Quatuor pou la fin du temps* (see Chapter 22).

177 Three Compositions for Piano,
No. 1 (1947)
Milton Babbitt (b. 1916)

These pieces are intended for performance as a single unit.

Accidentals affect only those notes which they immediately precede, except when notes are tied (♩ ♩)

The sign ⌐ ⌐ denotes the duration of *una corda*.

The following tempi may be substituted for those indicated in the first and third compositions: 96 instead of 108, and 112 instead of 126.

0:39.35

1:08.4

The row for the first of Milton Babbitt's *Three Compositions for Piano* (1947) is combinatorial: its two hexachords (that is, its first six and six notes) can be combined with one of the hexachords of an inverted, retrograde, or retrograde inverted form of the same row without producing any duplication of pitches. Here, P-0 is combinatorial with R-6. In other words, hexachord A of P-0 combines with hexachord B of R-6 to produce all twelve pitches. The order of the pitches is different from that in P-0, but combinatoriality is concerned only with the content of the individual (and combined) hexachords, not the actual sequence of the pitches. The complementary hexachords of the two forms (hexachord B of P-0 and hexachord A of R-6) are also combinatorial.

Example 12 Row forms used in Babbitt's *Three Compositions for Piano*, No. 1

Combinatoriality allowed composers to align different set-forms to sound at the same time without risking simultaneous or nearly simultaneous iterations of the same pitch-class. By exploiting the combinatorial properties of this row, Babbitt and others were able to create multiple statements of the twelve-tone row not only horizontally (in individual voices) but also vertically through the alignment of two different forms of the row sounding simultaneously. In the opening measures of the *Three Compositions for Piano,* No. 1, for example, we find the basic row both horizontally and vertically:

- Horizontally: the left hand in m. 1–2 presents P-0 in its entirety; the right hand presents P-6 in its entirety.
- Vertically: taking both voices together, all twelve pitches appear in m. 1; all twelve appear again in m. 2; in m. 3, and so on.

This same work also represents one of the earliest manifestations of integral serialism. In addition to manipulating the combinatorial properties of the row, Babbitt serializes the elements of rhythm, dynamics, and register as well. Using the sixteenth note as the unit of measure, he establishes a basic pattern of 5, 1, 4, 2 (that is, five sixteenth notes, followed by one sixteenth note, and so on) and "inverts" the rhythmic structure by subtracting these values from 6. Thus the rhythmic "matrix" of the work looks like this:

$$P = 5, 1, 4, 2 \qquad I = 1, 5, 2, 4$$
$$R = 2, 4, 1, 5 \qquad RI = 4, 2, 5, 1$$

Prime forms of the pitch row, regardless of the transposition, are always presented in the P rhythm (5, 1, 4, 2), inverted forms of the pitch row in the I rhythm (1, 5, 2, 4), retrograde inverted forms in the RI rhythm, and retrograde forms in the R rhythm. Rhythmic durations are articulated by disrupting the pattern of continuous sixteenth notes, either through rests or through slurred notes that create rhythms of longer duration. The grouping of 5 in the left hand in m. 1, for example, is created by the added duration on the note that comes fifth after the four initial sixteenth notes, whereas the subsequent "1" is articulated through the eighth-note rest at the end of m. 1.

TABLE OF PREPARATIONS

TONE		MATERIAL	STRINGS LEFT TO RIGHT	DISTANCE FROM DAMPER (IN INCHES)	MATERIAL	STRINGS LEFT TO RIGHT	DISTANCE FROM DAMPER (IN INCHES)
under	over	bamboo strips (½ in. wide)		½			
under	over	bamboo strips (½ in. wide)		2½-3			
under	over	bamboo strips (½ in. wide)		4- 4½			
		screw with 2 nuts	1-2	2 from bridge	bolt	2-3	1½ from bridge
		screw with 2 nuts	1-2	2¼	bolt	2-3	2
		screw with 2 nuts	1-2	2	bolt	2-3	1
		screw	1-2	2¼	hook screw	2-3	2½
		screw	1-2	1	screw with 2 nuts	2-3	2

OUR SPRING WILL COME

JOHN CAGE
(1943)

0:21.4

rit. poco a

poco e dim.

Tempo (152)

1:01

1:53.88

2:29

3:19

No. 178 Cage: *Our Spring Will Come*   ■   **573**

Our Spring Will Come was written by Cage for choreographer Pearl Primus and received its premiere in New York in 1944. Using a technique he had first used in another work for dance (*Bacchanale,* 1940), Cage "prepared" the piano that embodied the entire "orchestra." There are three types of preparation: bamboo strips weaving in and out of adjacent strings (from C♭ to C♭1), a combination of screws (with two nuts to hold them in place) and bolts (for F1, Ab1, and E2), and a combination of a single screw with two other types (G 2, C 3). There are thus 20 prepared notes, plus two unprepared pitches (A3, A1).

The score of *Our Spring Will Come*, like other works for prepared piano, reveals everything but the sounds actually heard (except for the unprepared A's), which run the gamut between the sound of a dampered piece of metal being struck and a gamelan-like ring. Like Renaissance and Baroque scores for lute and organ; a prepared piano score is more a tablature (telling a performer how to play) rather than a score (telling a listener what will be heard). The rapid, noncontrapuntal writing in *Our Spring Will Come* is disrupted by sections with *forzando* thuds on the lowest piano pitch, repetitive figures accompanied by A's (= 440) of long duration (although they are usually struck "quietly"), or nothing—two brief total silences. It may seem incongruous now that the score could be danced to, even if the choreography was considered radical (Primus "grunted and hummed, whispered, sang, and spoke as she gave herself to movement") while actor Gordon Heath read the eponymous poem by Langston Hughes on the condition of African Americans in the United States. But in Heath's opinion, Cage's music proved "an uncannily percussive equivalent of Pearl's dialogue with herself. I marveled and enunciated my narration warily."

179 Dripsody (1955)
Hugh Le Caine (1914–1977)

CD15, Track 4

Book p. 591

The Canadian composer Hugh Le Caine's *Dripsody* derives entirely from the briefest moment of sound: a single drop of water. In Le Caine's words: "A metal waste-basket was filled to a depth of two inches with water and water was allowed to drop from an eye-dropper held at a level of about ten feet from the basket. . . . To simplify the problem of composition, the simplest and most formless sound was chosen. . . . [The sound] was spliced onto a tape loop. . . . The rhythmic figures, which imitate rhythms of dripping water, were written down in musical notation. . . . Beneath each note in the written record was an intensity figure for that note, in decibels. The time values of the notes were translated into tape-lengths. . . . [A]ll the operations which are easily done on a tape recorder were used. . . . Four tape loops were set up, including the original loop. . . . By printing various combinations of the four loops at three different speeds at the same time, the effect of 12 tape loops was obtained without any further splicing. . . .In the arpeggio section, a single arpeggio of twelve notes was spliced up. . . . The next effect then involved a number of arpeggios, both upward and downward, at various pitches and speeds, played at the same time. . . . With only 25 splices actually made, the result of using tape techniques is to produce a final record in which thousands of independent sounds are heard." [1]

By running the recording of the drop of water over and over again through a variable-speed tape recorder, Le Caine was able to create an astonishing variety of sounds never before heard. But the work is far more than interesting sonic effects: it has a definite shape, a trajectory that projects a sense of drama and development. The ending of the work plays on the sound of the proverbial dripping faucet, leaving the unsuspecting listener uncertain just when the work has ended.

[1]Quoted in Gayle Young, *The Sackbut Blues: Hugh Le Caine, Pioneer in Electronic Music* (Ottawa, ON: National Museum of Science and Technology, 1989), 90–91.

575

180 In C (1964)
Terry Riley (b. 1935)

CD15, Track 5
Book p. 600

IN C
Performing Directions

All performers play from the same page of 53 melodic patterns played in sequence.

Any number of any kind of instruments can play. A group of about 35 is desired if possible but smaller or larger groups will work. If vocalist(s) join in they can use any vowel and consonant sounds they like.

Patterns are to be played consecutively with each performer having the freedom to determine how many times he or she will repeat each pattern before moving on to the next. There is no fixed rule as to the number of repetitions a pattern may have, however, since performances normally average between 45 minutes and an hour and a half, it can be assumed that one would repeat each pattern from somewhere between 45 seconds and a minute and a half or longer.

It is very important that performers listen very carefully to one another and this means occasionally to drop out and listen. As an ensemble, it is very desireable to play very softly as well as very loudly and to try to diminuendo and crescendo together.

Each pattern can be played in unison or canonically in any alignment with itself or with its neighboring patterns. One of the joys of IN C is the interaction of the players in polyrhythmic combinations that spontaneously arise between patterns. Some quite fantastic shapes will arise and disintegrate as the group moves through the piece when it is properly played.

It is important not to hurry from pattern to pattern but to stay on a pattern long enough to interlock with other patterns being played. As the performance progresses, performers should stay within 2 or 3 patterns of each other. It is important not to race too far ahead or to lag too far behind.

The ensemble can be aided by the means of a 1/8 note pulse played played on the high c's of the piano or on a mallet instrument. It is also possible to use improvised percussion in strict rhythm (drum set, cymbals bells etc.), if it is carefully done and doesn't overpower the ensemble. All performers must play strictly in rhythm and it is essential that every one play each pattern carefully. It is advised to rehearse patterns in unison before attempting to play the piece to determine that everyone is playing correctly.

(continued on p. 564)

The tempo is left to the discretion of the performers. Obviously, not too slow but it should not be faster than performers can comfortably play.

It is important to think of patterns periodically so that when you are resting you are conscious of the larger periodic composite accents that are sounding and when you re-enter you are aware of what effect your entrance will have on the musics flow.

The group should aim to merge into a unison at least once or twice during the performance. At the same time if the players seem to be consistently too much in the same alignment of a pattern try shifting your alignment by an 1/8th note or quarter note with what's going on in the rest of the ensemble.

It is OK to transpose patterns by an octave, especially to transpose up. Transposing down by octaves works best on the patterns containing notes of long durations. Augmentation of rhythmic values can also be effective.

If a performer comes to a pattern that for some reason can't be played--just omit it and go on.

Instruments can be amplified if desired. Electronic keyboards are welcome also.

In C is ended in this way: When each performer arrives at figure #53 he or she stays on it until the entire ensemble has arrived there. The group then makes a large crescendo and diminuendo a few times and then each player drops out as he or she wishes.

Terry Riley

A strategy based on repetition and gradual change is at work in one of the earliest of all minimalist works, Terry Riley's *In C* (1964). The score consists of 53 brief thematic fragments to be played in any combination of any kind of instruments, though the composer recommends a group of about 35 if possible. Each player performs these ideas in the same sequence but is free to repeat each unit as often as he or she sees fit. "There is no fixed rule as to the number of repetitions a pattern may have," the composer notes in the score, though if a performance runs between 45 and 90 minutes, then each performer would ordinarily repeat each pattern for somewhere between 40 and 90 seconds. "One of the joys of *In C*," the composer noted in his performing directions to the score, "is the interaction of the players in polyrhythmic combinations that spontaneously arise between patterns. Some quite fantastic shapes will arise and disintegrate as the group moves through the piece when it is properly played." The one constant element of the piece is an ostinato C octave played on the high range of a piano or mallet instrument. If a performance of *In C* runs to 90 minutes, this would mean repeating this particular figure as many as 15,000 times in succession. While this might sound like a recipe for monotony, the process of unfolding is such that the work remains constantly in motion and gradually transforms itself into whatever the performers decide it will become.

What kind of a work is *In C*? It resists classification. It bears many hallmarks of jazz (individual "riffs," enormous latitude for improvisation), yet it is essentially a canon at the unison. Riley notes that "all performers must play strictly in rhythm," and he even recommends that musicians "rehearse patterns in unison before attempting to play the piece to determine that everyone is playing correctly." In many respects, *In C* harks back to an earlier period of time—its open-ended instrumentation and the tremendous latitude given to performers seem in some respects more typical of the Renaissance or Baroque eras than the 20th century. "At the time I wrote *In C*, I was almost ready to drop out of music," the composer once explained. "Classical music was very mental; the mind governed the musical activity. I think the shift in what this music [*In C*] was doing was letting the heart back into the game. I wanted to make the score so minimal that it wasn't important anymore."

Performance notes: Terry Riley has recorded *In C* on several occasions. The best known are those made in 1968 with Members of the New Music Center at the State University of New York, Buffalo, and the "25th Anniversary Recording" made in San Francisco in 1990. Not surprisingly, given the nature of this music, the two performances are quite different. The earlier was performed by an ensemble of 11 musicians and runs 43 minutes. The later recording, with an ensemble of 31 musicians, runs 76 minutes. It is from the first of these performances that the excerpt here has been taken. In 1989, Riley supervised a recording by the Shangai Film Orchestra on Chinese instruments. An unexpected difficulty occurred: the musicians "rushed" through the 53 fragments so quickly that the piece was ready to end in just over 10 minutes; to compensate, the conductor brought back earlier fragments to extend the piece. Other ensembles have recorded the work as well. A group called Piano Circus has recorded a version entirely on keyboard instruments that runs 20 minutes; and a 2002 electronic realization by the European Music Project is affectionately known as the "disco version" of *In C*.

hold tempo 1 / Tempo 1 fortsetzen / tenir le tempo 1.

* The piece may be played an octave lower than written, when played on marimbas. / Wenn Marimbas verwendet werden, kann das Stück eine Oktave tiefer als notiert gespielt werden. / La pièce pourra être jouée à l'octave inférieure quand elle est exécutée par des marimbas.

a.v.s. = accelerando very slightly. / sehr geringfügiges accelerando. / très légèrement accelerando.

1967

L1/80

UE 16156 L

Reproduced and printed by
Halstan & Co. Ltd., Amersham, Bucks., England

One manifestation of minimalism involves what has come to be known as phase music or process music, in which one can clearly hear the process by which the elements of a work gradually transform themselves into something new and different. In the 1960s and early 1970s, Steve Reich applied this principle to musique concrète works, music for live performers interacting with electronics, and works for live performers. *Piano Phase* for two pianos or two marimbas (1967) is an early example of the last kind of minimalism, in which a series of measures (or modules) are played through by two musicians, slightly out of phase with one another. Reich thought a performance would last around 20 minutes.

Both pianists play in the same range throughout (E 1 up to D 2, ending on A1 up to E2). The piece is in three sections:

The parts begin by alternating two- (a fifth, on E1) and three-note (a fifth and minor third, on F♯1) to produce a 12-note ostinato figure; the tonal effect is of a Dorian mode on E. Opening solo, the first performer (Reich's term) holds a steady tempo through the first 25 of 32 modules. Each module is repeated a predetermined number of times within a specified range. Once the first performer has established the steady state, the second performer takes the same interlocking ostinato figure, but "accelerates very slightly" between each module (each acceleration will itself take several repetitions by the first performer). By the end of each accelerating module, the second performer is to be one sixteenth "ahead" of the first performer. Twelve modular shifts are necessary before the unison returns. Once more the second performer drops out and the figure continues.

When the second performer reenters, its ostinato changes the ascending fifth to an ascending fourth (right hand), while the left hand changes the B1 to A1 and plays a 8-note ostinato. The shifting pattern begins again, although the process now takes only 8 modules—but Reich starts asking for a larger number of repetitions per module, ranging from 16 to 32 times (versus 12 to 24 times in the first section).

In the third and final section, the second performer takes the lead initially before the first performer reenters. The ostinato is down to four notes, in what may be heard as a four-note scale on A1. The phasing again returns to the second performer's part, but it requires only 4 modules before unison is reachieved, although Reich again "compensates" for the shorter modular shift by increasing the number of repetitions to as many as 60. Once the 32nd and final module is satisfactorily achieved, the performers cue to end.

Piano Phase is essentially a canon at the unison, but the element of tempo has become the primary compositional process, putting the canon through a subtle time warp. As Reich directs the performers, the point "is not to count repeats, but to listen to the two voice relationship and as you hear it clearly and have absorbed it, move on to the next bar."

182 Orfeo II (excerpt) (1976)
Thea Musgrave (b. 1928)

CD15, Track 7

Book p. 605

NOTES ON PERFORMANCE

Orfeo II is projected as a ballet for solo male dancer, although it can equally well be performed in concert form. The dancer takes the part of Orfeo, as does the solo flute. All other elements are represented by the orchestra — they are invisible: their presence is indicated by lighting effects, or laser beam projections etc. Orfeo's journey to the Underworld exists only in his imagination.

The flautist should also be on-stage (he is to some extent Orfeo's *alter ego*) and there should be close interaction between him and the dancer (though, of course, he is 'invisible' to the dancer). The principal 1st violin represents Euridice (that is, heard not seen) and so, in concert version, the player should sit at the back, hidden by the other players.

The solo flute should play with considerable rubato independently of the conductor. Where there are arrows synchronization must be exact, otherwise there can be some flexibility. Adjust tempo so that synchronization is *approximately* as written.

Accidentals in *unmeasured* bars apply only to the note they precede, except where one note or a pair of notes is immediately repeated.

↓ represents downbeat to an unmeasured bar: here, the music should continue in the same tempo (unless otherwise marked), though with rubato.

This work also exists in another version — *Orfeo I* for flute and pre-recorded tape. Like *Orfeo II*, this is projected as a ballet, but is equally suited to concert performance.

SCENARIO

1 Orfeo laments.

Orfeo stands alone on the banks of the river Styx and grieves for Euridice. He hears a distant echo of her voice and he listens. Then it disappears. Orfeo in despair pleads with Charon to ferry him across the river so that he may search for her.

2 Orfeo crosses the river Styx.

Charon consents to listen to his plea. The waves of the river begin to ripple and then surge up and part, and Orfeo can cross to the other side.

3 Orfeo calms the Furies.

Orfeo is confronted by the Furies, and eloquently he pleads with them. They gradually quieten as they listen. He is allowed to proceed, but on one condition...that he must not look at Euridice till he has returned to the other side of the river.

4 Orfeo searches amongst the Shades.

Orfeo searches for Euridice amongst the Shades. He hears her approaching... he steps towards her, then turns away and shields his eyes.

5 Orfeo hears Euridice's pleas.

Orfeo hears Euridice pleading with him to turn and look at her...he cannot resist and he turns. Euridice vanishes for ever.

6 Orfeo is attacked by the Bacchantes.

Orfeo is at once attacked violently by the Bacchantes. He makes a last desperate plea, but he finds himself back on the banks of the river Styx, alone and desolate.

1:25.4

2:58.8

Thea Musgrave's *Orfeo II,* scored for solo flute and 15 strings, moves freely between tonal and atonal idioms. Long passages of its opening section ("Orfeo Laments") are centered on G and D. It would be misleading to say the music is "in" either of these keys, but it has a strong sense of a tonal center. The tonality is reinforced rhythmically by the steady, repeated pattern of eighth notes in the opening in the lower voices, almost in the fashion of a Baroque ground bass.

At figure 4, the first violin intones the opening phrase of the most famous aria from Christoph Willibald Gluck's opera *Orfeo* of 1762, *Che farò senza Euridice?* ("What shall I do without Euridice?"), Orpheus's moving lament at the loss of his beloved wife (Example 23-2). This reminiscence from another musical world—the middle of the 18th century—has an eerie effect within the context of Musgrave's *Orfeo II.* When it appears in the first violin at figure 4, it sounds like (and is) a fleeting memory. The flute soloist, representing Orpheus, listens to the fragments of this melody and tries to imitate them (just after figure 10 through figure 14) but cannot sustain the line. Orpheus's inability to recover the tonal melody parallels his inability to recover the dead Eurydice.

Example 13 Gluck, *Orfeo ed Euridice, Che farò senza Euridice?*

What shall I do without Euridice? Where shall I go without my beloved?

As in Ives's *Unanswered Question* (Anthology 2/154) and Schoenberg's "O alter Duft" from *Pierrot lunaire* (Anthology 2/160), Musgrave juxtaposes tonal and nontonal harmonies to create a sense of tonality that nevertheless sounds strangely discordant.

~ 14 ~

attacca mv't III

References to past idioms, although frequently used in postmodern music, are not essential to its aesthetic. But what happens when modernism confronts popular music in the same work? Tania León's *A la par*, a three-movement work for percussion (including piano), offers one possible scenario. The second movement, "Guaguancó," mixes the rhythms of a Cuban popular dance with atonal harmonies. León calls this her attempt "to express the dichotomy between the folk-music traditions of my native Cuba and the Classical European training I received at the Havana Conservatory." In this particular movement, the repeated melodic-rhythmic figure in the bass line seems to represent the vernacular idioms of Cuban dance (specifically the Afro-Cuban dance known as the *guaguancó*) while the other instrumental lines reflect the idiom of European modernism.

The work's title translates loosely as "at the same time as" or "on a par with," a fitting description of the relationship between popular and modernist styles here. Even though they are often quite distinct—each goes its own way—they nevertheless complement one another to create a whole larger than the sum of its parts. Every instrument seems to occupy its own space, yet in the end, everything is indeed *a la par*. As a work of postmodernism, León's *A la par*, is both tonal and atonal, rhythmically regular and irregular, serious and playful. It represents instead the increasing tendency of music in the late 20th century toward a synthesis of diverse styles and traditions.

184 **Seven Magnificat Antiphons** (1988, 1991):
No. 1 ("O Weisheit")
Arvo Pärt (b. 1935)

CD15, Track 9

Book p. 608

1. O Weisheit

Universal Edition UE 19098

UE 19098

1:11.75

While Debussy, Gershwin, and León turned to popular music for inspiration, others have turned to a much earlier era. Arvo Pärt, born in Estonia, wrote music using serialist and other modernist techniques during the early part of his career. After the unpredictability of official Soviet reactions led the composer to establish a pattern of lengthy compositional silences interrupted by bursts of activity, Pärt, who had delved into medieval and Renaissance vocal music as well as plainchant, discovered the concept of *tintinnabuli* (Latin, small bells). If plainchant could be heard as perfect unity (or, metaphorically, a stream of light), the simple triad was the most perfect realization of that unity when sent through a prism, revealing all colors: "The three notes of a triad are like bells. And that's why I call it tintinnabulation." For Pärt, this was a way to cope with "the complex and multifaceted," which "only confuses" him.

Although a score like "O Weisheit" ("O Wisdom," addressed to God) from the *Seven Magnificat-Antiphons* (chamber choir, 1988, revised 1991) seems simple, even monolithic in character, the music has analyzable elements, both ancient and modern: a relatively slow tempo, two durational values (half and whole note), harmony revolving around A major (although, when the lowest voices enter, the chord is in second inversion), and alternation between full 8-note chords (dividing each section in half) and 4-note chords (altos and tenors only). Phrasing of the text (the first of the Advent antiphons, sung before the Magnificat itself) is accomplished by one-measure rests.

The piece is indeed about unity, but the changing pitches (also in the middle voices) generate changes in overtones (much as a bell continues to vibrate after being struck, which is heard as pitch change). Although this is chant-like, there is no melody per se; the voice leading is now less complex than early organum; and the dynamics are strictly *piano*, the only change occurring with the choral texture changes. "O Weisheit" is the first of seven short pieces; the complexities will expand gradually through the cycle, but the tintinnabular approach remains the essence of this and other Pärt works. He is not "rediscovering" the wheel of consonance; he is changing our perspective on it.

O Weisheit,
hervorgegangen aus dem Munde des
Höchsten,
die Welt umspannst du von einem Ende
zum andern,
in Kraft und Milde ordnest du alles:
O komm und offenbare uns den Weg der
Weisheit und der Einsicht.
O Weisheit.

O Wisdom,
proceeding from the mouth of the Highest,

you encompass the world from one end to
the other,
in power and mildness you regulate all:
O come and reveal to us the path of
wisdom and insight.
O Wisdom.

Maple Leaf Rag (1899)

Scott Joplin (1868–1917)

CD15, Track 10

Book p. 619

Tempo di marcia

1:46.7

Ragtime first flourished in the United States at the end of the 19th century and in the early decades of the 20th. It grew out of the confluence of the largely unwritten tradition of African-American dance, minstrel dance (particularly the cakewalk), and such ballroom dances as the two-step and polka. Joplin's enormously popular *Maple Leaf Rag* exemplifies the style: it is in duple meter and based on units of eight or sixteen measures. Syncopation is prevalent throughout, thrown into relief by the steadiness of the bass line typically heard in the banjo music of minstrel shows (see Chapter 16). The *Maple Leaf Rag* is also typical in that it follows the basic form of a march: three or four different themes, each running to sixteen measures, with connecting material between sections. In ragtime, the opening theme is often repeated after the second theme. Formally, *Maple Leaf Rag* follows the typical ragtime pattern of AA BB A CC DD.

Performance notes: This performance is from a piano roll recording made by the composer himself in 1916. Piano rolls were coiled rolls of punched paper, each punch corresponding to a particular key on a piano specially made or adapted to play these rolls. Piano rolls enjoyed their greatest vogue in the 1910s and 1920s. One important drawback of this medium was that it could not reproduce gradiations of volume; thus Joplin's recording here conveys no sense of difference between loud or soft. Still, the performance helps capture some sense of how the composer performed his own music. Embellishments and slight variations abound throughout, particularly when a given section is being repeated.

186 **Children's Corner Suite:** "Golliwog's
Cakewalk" (1908)
Debussy

0:58.5

2:12.3

No. 186 Debussy: *Children's Corner Suite* ■ **593**

The text block at bottom left:

Debussy wrote his *Children's Corner Suite* (1908) for his daughter Emma (affectionately known as "Chou Chou"). The English title and movement titles reflect the language of the child's governess, a Miss Gibbs. The last movement of the suite, "Golliwog's Cakewalk," captures the syncopated rhythms of the cakewalk, a strutting dance that figured prominently in minstrel shows of the day. Debussy adds a touch of irony to his work by incorporating into it (m. 61–63) an oblique reference to the celebrated "Tristan chord" of Wagner's *Tristan und Isolde* (see Anthology 2/139a). He instructs the performer to play this passage haltingly, and "with great emotion," only to answer the quotation with a series of jaunty, disjointed eighth notes.

187 St. Louis Blues (1914)
W. C. Handy (1873–1958)

CD15, Track 12
Book p. 622

Words and Music by
W. C. HANDY

1. I hate to see___ de ev'- nin' sun go down,___
2. Been to de Gyp-sy to get ma for - tune tole,___
You ought to see___ dat stove-pipe brown of mine,___

Hate to see___ de ev'- nin' sun go down,___
To de Gyp-sy done got ma for - tune tole,___
Lak he owns___ de Di-mon Jos - eph line,___

Copyright 1914 by W. C. Handy; copyright renewed

St. Louis Blues is constructed on a standard pattern known as the 12-bar blues form. This consists of a series of variations on a repeated harmonic pattern of 12 measures in 4/4 time. Each of these 12-measure units is known generically as a chorus and is in turn divided into three groups of four measures each. The harmonic progression in *St. Louis Blues* follows a harmonic pattern typical for the blues:

Measure number	1 2 3 4	5 6 7 8	9 10 11 12
Harmony	I	IV I	V I

Like a great many blues numbers, *St. Louis Blues* opens with a vamp, a short progression of chords (and in this particular case, a melody as well) whose function is to introduce the basic harmonies, tempo, and mood of the whole. The vamp in *St. Louis* Blues is unusual in that it contrasts markedly with the chorus that follows. Handy explained this unusual feature in his autobiography:

> When *St. Louis Blues* was written the tango was in vogue. I tricked the dancers by arranging a tango introduction, breaking abruptly then into a low-down blues. My eyes swept the floor anxiously, then suddenly I saw lightning strike. The dancers seemed electrified. Something within them came suddenly to life. An instinct that wanted so much to live, to fling its arms and to spread joy, took them by the heels. By this I was convinced that my new song was accepted.[1]

But the notated score gives only the barest of outlines for what the blues actually sound like in performance. As with *basse danse* forms of the Renaissance (see Chapters 5 and 6), the basic structure leaves room for enormous variation. Harmonies can be altered, enriched, or made to move at a faster speed, and melodies can easily be changed to accommodate the text. In performance, a blues song is fluid in spite of its underlying form. The same work can be realized in strikingly different ways.

A classic collaboration on a recording of W. C. Handy's St. Louis Blues illustrates the extraordinary flexibility not only of the blues, but of jazz in general. When Bessie Smith (1895–1937) recorded this number in 1925 with the trumpeter Louis Armstrong, she omitted the vamp and altered many of the words in Handy's published score. The melodic line in this performance often bears only the faintest resemblance to the notated melody: Smith's plaintive sound and the slow tempo create something more nearly akin at times to speech. The simplicity of the arrangement—a reed organ (harmonium) provides the only accompaniment—focuses attention on the ongoing dialogue of the two soloists: Armstrong's mournful trumpet responds to each phrase of Smith's singing. This recording, which was marketed by Columbia as a "race record" (that is, music recorded by and intended for African Americans), helped further solidify Smith's reputation as "Empress of the Blues" and helped make her the highest-paid African-American entertainer in the United States at the time.

St. Louis Blues the notated score gives only the barest of outlines for what the blues actually sound like in performance; the treatment of pitch by blues and jazz performers, for example, is virtually unnotatable.

[1] W. C. Handy, *Father of the Blues: An Autobiography*, ed. Arna Bontemps (New York: Macmillan, 1941), p. 122.

Piano Prelude *#2* (1926)
George Gershwin (1898–1937)

CD15, Track 13
Book p. 624

Prelude II
(Blue Lullaby)
(1926)

By GEORGE GERSHWIN
Edited by ALICIA ZIZZO

*OSSIA: Do not break chords. On third beat, play B♯ with R.H.

PF0895

Largamente con moto
Optional: REVERSE HANDS

slightly jazzy

Tempo I

1:32.79

*OSSIA: Slightly accelerate ending

Elements of the blues, notably the emphasis on certain scale pitches and the "bending" of pitch, soon became part of other musical genres. Jazz counted on blues as one of the crucial sources of its development. Composers of dance and theater music also incorporated these elements. But the most versatile of these composers, who brought the crossover blend of blues, early jazz, and "concert hall" music to a peak of popularity, was George Gershwin, who began his career as a Tin Pan Alley song-plugger and writer. He began to write piano pieces, songs for other shows, hit songs ("Swanee," 1919), and musicals, mostly with his brother Ira (1896–1983). Gershwin also wrote large-scale works with orchestra reflecting the crossover style, including *Rhapsody in Blue, Concerto in F, An American in Paris,* and the opera *Porgy and Bess.*

Among Gershwin's piano solos are the Three Preludes, composed and premiered in 1926 by the composer. He actually composed five preludes, but two were eliminated before publication. (In fact, Gershwin had planned for a set of 24 preludes, after the examples of Bach and, more specifically, Chopin.) The second prelude, *Andante con moto e poco rubato* in E major, was described by Gershwin as a "blues lullaby"; a comparison with Chopin's prelude in A minor, op. 28, no. 2 (Anthology 2/129) shows that this piece is essentially an homage to the Polish master.

189 **Night and Day** (1932)
Cole Porter (1891–1964)

CD15, Track 14
Book p. 624

Songs like Porter's *Night and Day* and Ellington's *Sophisticated Lady* reflect the traditions of the 19th-century *Lied* in remarkable ways. The harmonic vocabularies of these works, although essentially tonal, are richly chromatic and far from straightforward. The poetry is elegant and witty, the melodies unforgettable, and the union of the two represents the genre at its best. In Porter's *Night and Day,* the juxtaposition of the wandering chromatic line in the bass against the repeated B♭ of the voice establishes the underlying tension between longing and insistency. Finally, after 35 iterations of B♭, the vocal line itself begins to rise and fall chromatically, gradually, languorously: the longing has become infectious. We do not feel a strong sense of tonic until the word "one" in the clinching phrase ". . . you are the one" (m. 23). In m. 52, the music moves to a remote key (G♭ = ♭III), the repeated notes grow into a back-and-forth a whole step (m. 57), and the tonic finally returns after a circuitous passage through a series of chromatic harmonies. Unlike Wagner in Act II of *Tristan und Isolde* (Anthology 2/139b), or Leonard Bernstein in the Quintet "Tonight" from *West Side Story* (Anthology 2/173), Porter erases the differences between night and day: the lover here is indifferent to the setting and rising of the sun.

Like many songs of this era, *Night and Day* has been subjected to countless arrangements, vocal and instrumental. It was first recorded by Fred Astaire for the movie *The Gay Divorcee* (1934), a comedy that revolves around mistaken identity and provides a platform for much singing and dancing. Within three months of the film's premiere, more than 30 artists had recorded the song. Within 25 years, the number had surpassed a hundred. And no two recordings are alike: the performance tradition of a song like *Night and Day* allows—and in fact encourages—performers to take considerable liberties with its rhythm, text, orchestration, harmonies, words, and even its melody. Frank Sinatra's version sounds very different from Ella Fitzgerald's, which in turn sounds very different from Fred Astaire's. Nor can any of these renditions really be said to represent the composer's original intentions, because Cole Porter did not really conceive of the song as a fixed entity. The notion of an "authentic" version of this song is in fact vaguely ridiculous. Is it Cole Porter's original manuscript? The first edition? The first recording? As in jazz, improvisatory freedom plays such a basic role in this kind of music that the idea of an authentic text loses all relevance.

190 **Sophisticated Lady** (1933)

Duke Ellington (1899–1974)

CD15, Track 15

Book p. 624

Ellington's *Sophisticated Lady* uses advanced melodic and harmonic chromaticism to project the idea of a woman who has assumed a worldly attitude toward life and love. This chromaticism as well as the rhythmic freedom of Sarah Vaughan's interpretation emphasize the woman's exterior life of glamour and uncaring attitude ("Smoking, drinking, never thinking of tomorrow, nonchalant . . ."). Only with the final word of the text—"cry"—does the music arrive at its long-avoided resolution on the tonic. The chromaticism, in the end, is revealed as a mask covering the woman's true feelings.

191 Snake Rag (1923)
Joe Oliver (1885–1938)

CD15, Track 16

Book p. 628

Louis Armstrong (1901–1971) began his career in his home town of New Orleans. He joined the exodus of jazz musicians to Chicago in 1923, working for the band of fellow cornettist, Joe "King" Oliver. Armstrong and Oliver developed an intricate duet style, sounding improvised but in fact carefully worked out. This was an important new element of jazz: increasing emphasis on arrangement while continuing to delight in improvisational skill. This recording of Oliver's "Snake Rag," recorded in 1923, includes Lil Hardin (Armstrong's future wife) on piano, Honore Dutrey on trombone (with its *glissando* interjections), Bud Scott on banjo, and the Dodds brothers (Johnny on clarinet, Baby on drums). Much like Sousa's *King Cotton* (Anthology 2/144), the piece modulates to the subdominant in midstream, without returning to the original key.

Armstrong moved to New York in 1924, switched to trumpet, and played with the Fletcher Henderson Orchestra and Clarence Williams (with whom he backed Bessie Smith on "St. Louis Blues"; Anthology 2/187). He returned to Chicago to begin leading his own groups, the Hot Five and Hot Seven; as the primary soloist, Armstrong recorded solos of considerable virtuosity and inventiveness, and his reputation as the greatest jazz soloist of his era was firmly established. From then on, he moved between Chicago and New York, joining the pit orchestra for Fats Waller's 1929 *Hot Chocolates* and recording the show's hit, "Ain't Misbehavin'" (Anthology 2/172). By 1930, "Louis Armstrong and His Orchestra" was the ensemble (usually 10 or so musicians) in which he made his continuing contributions to jazz.

192 It Don't Mean a Thing (If It Ain't Got that Swing) (1930)
Duke Ellington (1899–1974)

CD15, Track 17

Book p. 628

Duke Ellington's *It Don't Mean a Thing (If It Ain't Got that Swing)* represents jazz in the "Swing" era of the 1930s and 1940s. Swing rhythm features a hard meter but a subtle avoidance of cadences and downbeats, with the soloist placing notes either just ahead or just behind the beat in a way that heightened the music's rhythmic suppleness. Formally, the original song version of Ellington's *It Don't Mean a Thing* consists of an eight-measure instrumental introduction, followed by a two-measure vamp, a short progression of chords that can be repeated indefinitely before the entrance of the voice. The verse ("What good is melody . . .") consists of 16 measures (2 × 8) that end on a half cadence leading to the song's chorus or principal melody. The chorus itself consists of four units of eight measures, the thematic content of each following the pattern AABA. This pattern is so common in 20th-century song that it has come to be known as song form. The contrasting B section (here, from the words "It makes no diff'rence" through "ev'rything you got") is often known as the bridge because it connects statements of the A theme.

Performance notes: When Ellington recorded this number with his band in 1932, he substantially reworked the form of the piece. The recorded version omits the introduction and begins with ten measures of the vamp, in which the singer (Ivie Anderson) uses her voice as an instrument, singing syncopated nonsense syllables against the steady beat of the bass in a technique known as scat singing. The 32-measure verse, expanded from the song's 16-measure version, is allotted to a solo muted trombone. The voice, in turn, presents the chorus in its full 32-measure form. At this point, the instruments take over with a series of quasi-improvised solos. In rehearsal, Ellington and his group would have planned who would play these solos and in what order, but, beyond this, each instrumentalist was free to improvise at will, knowing in advance the basic chord progressions with which the band would support him. In this particular performance, we hear only one extended solo, given to the saxophonist (Johnny Hodges), who varies thematic elements of both verse and chorus. The full band then plays the opening of the chorus; the vocalist returns with the bridge passage, and the work concludes with the syncopated "doo-wah" fragmented on the muted brass. Other performances of this same work by Ellington vary the number and sequence of the soloists, the order in which verse and chorus are first presented, the final cadence, and countless other features large and small. Jazz performances by their very nature represent a fusion of composed and improvised elements.

CD15, Track 18
Book p. 632

BLUE IN GREEN

By MILES DAVIS

1:42.68

2:23.85

3:05.67

3:26.1

In the decade after World War II, a new style of jazz called bebop came to the fore; it featured fast tempos, irregular chordal progressions, complex harmonies, and asymmetrical, often jagged melodies. In some cases, both musicians also incorporated elements of what came to be known as Afro-Cuban jazz, with an expanded percussion section and an emphasis on ostinato figures and complex polyrhythms. In contradiction to the mood of the times, Miles Davis's album *The Birth of the Cool* (1949) featured a style in which vibrato in the winds was held to a minimum, creating a distinctively "cool" sound that avoided the sentimentality and fullness so characteristic of the swing era.

But Davis was among those who, in the 1950s, helped develop a "modal" approach to jazz improvisation, in which scales or harmonic patterns became the underpinning for improvisation, rather than existing songs or standard progressions. Instead of the pressure of bebop's harmonic complexities, soloists now had the opportunity to "stretch" out in improvisational exploration, rather than having to "exchange choruses" on a regular basis. With tape recording and the long-playing record now available, jazz recording gained new freedom, as it became possible to structure an album conceptually, as a sequence of pieces. One result was Davis's *Kind of Blue*, which featured an all-star group of sidemen: saxophonists Julian "Cannonball" Adderly and John Coltrane, pianist Bill Evans, bassist Paul Chambers, drummer Jimmy Cobb, and (on one track) pianist Wynton Kelly.

Considering the prevalence of rapid-fire performances in bebop, it is noteworthy that tempos in the five compositions on *Kind of Blue* are described either as moderately" or "slowly." The most recognizable tracks are "All Blues," a relaxed blues in 6/4, and "So What," a call-and-response between the bass (a nine-note solo) and the others (a two-chord reply mimicking "So what?"), with a 32-measure cycling of two scales as an improvisational underpinning; there is also a fairly traditional blues number, "Freddie Freeloader." "Flamenco Sketches" is based on a repeated chord on C, while each soloist works through a series of five scales until finished.

In "Blue in Green" (recorded without Adderly or Kelly), after a four-bar introduction by Evans, a 10-measure progression of freely modal harmonies (starting and ending on A) serves as the basis upon which the soloists improvise (Davis twice through, Coltrane twice, Davis twice); this pattern alternates with Evans performing the progression transposed a whole step down (to G), which occurs after the first Davis set and the Coltrane set (now "double time, rubato"); after the second Davis set, Evans's transposed double-time rubato version is played through twice before a cadence on D (an echo of the piano introduction).

The relative rigor of "Blue in Green" (improvisation based on a modal chord progression) is an antidote to the freedom of "Flamenco Sketches" (improvisation based on an untimed series of scales); the combination of these more unusual pieces with two tunes with catchy riffs and an straightforward blues resulted in a record that has not only sold more than any other jazz album, but has had as much influence as any post–World War II jazz recording.

4:49.2

CD15, Track 19
Book p. 636

Foggy Mountain Breakdown

Words and Music by
EARL SCRUGGS

The instrumental version of *Foggy Mountain Breakdown* first recorded by Lester Flatt, Earl Scruggs, and the Foggy Mountain Boys in 1949, represents the country music subgenre of bluegrass. The style's name derives from the band in which Flatt and Scruggs first met, Bill Monroe and his Blue Grass Boys. The characteristic sound of bluegrass is an acoustic string ensemble of banjo (played by Scruggs), guitar (played by Flatt), fiddle, and double bass. The banjo is picked (as opposed to strummed), and vocals tend to be pitched in the upper end of the singer's register, creating what has been described as a "high, lonesome sound." The characteristic syncopation of bluegrass anticipates the downbeat slightly, in contrast to jazz, in which performers often play just slightly behind the beat. The resulting rhythms are propulsive and infectious—"folk music with overdrive" as one commentator described it.

In *Foggy Mountain Breakdown*, Scruggs demonstrates his renowned technique of three-finger banjo picking. The virtuosity is dazzling, even within the relatively simple harmonic and metrical confines of this particular number. The piece also reveals formal similarities with the basic patterns of many blues and jazz numbers: soloists take turns improvising variations on a given theme or harmonic pattern. Like jazz, bluegrass and other forms of country music provided performers with a framework for improvisation. As with songs by Porter, Ellington, Waller, and Berry, the sheet music is the product of a publisher's transcription for public consumption: based on a recording, this "score" is designed to convey the melody, words, harmonies, and rhythms, but not the overall arrangement.

195 Roll Over, Beethoven (1956)
Chuck Berry (b. 1926)

CD15, Track 20
Book p. 641

Chuck Berry's *Roll Over, Beethoven* is typical of many early rock-and-roll songs of the 1950s and early 1960s. Its melodic range is limited, its formal structure and rhythms repetitive, its essential harmonies confined to the tonic and subdominant—and for all these reasons, the work is mesmerizing. The lyrics themselves—urging the most revered of all classical composers to turn over in his grave—evoke a cultural war between "high" and "low" art, contemplation and activity, old and young. The song spoke directly to a generation of teenagers, and it retains its elemental force today. Formally, *Roll Over, Beethoven* follows the 12-bar blues form. The published lead sheet provides only the barest outline of the melody, harmonies, and words; a great many aspects of the music are left to the discretion of the performer or performers.

CREDITS

99. Georg Matthias Monn, Symphony in B major, first movement.

100. Domenico Scarlatti, Sonata in D Major, K. 492. From *Sixty Sonatas Vol. II* by Domenico Scarlatti. Edited by Ralph Kirkpatrick. Copyright © 1953 (renewed) by G. Schirmer, Inc. (ASCAP). International copyright secured. All rights reserved. Reprinted by permission.

101. Johann Stamitz, Symphony in D major, Op. 3, No.2, first movement.

102. Johann Christian Bach, Sonata in D major, Op. 5, No.2, first movement.

103. Carl Philipp Emanuel Bach, Fantasia in C minor (finale of Keyboard Sonata, Wq. 63/6). Reprinted with permission from Howard Ferguson, ed. *C.P.E. Bach, Selected Keyboard Works, Book 4.* © 1983 Associated Board of the Royal Schools of Music. Reproduced with permission.

104. Joseph Haydn, Piano Sonata in C Minor, Hob. XVI:20, first movement. Reprinted with permission of G. Henle Publishing from Georg Feder, ed., Joseph Haydn, *Werke,* Reihe XVIII, Bd. 2, Folge 2 (Munich: G. Henle, © 1970).

105. Joseph Haydn, String Quartet in C Major, Op. 33, No. 3—I. Allegro moderato II. Scherzo: Allegretto III. Adagio ma non troppo IV. Rondo: Presto. Reprinted with permission of G. Henle Publishing from Georg Feder, ed., Joseph Haydn, *Werke,* Reihe XII, Bd. 3. (Munich: G. Henle, © 1974.)

106. Joseph Haydn, Symphony No. 103 in E-flat Major, first movement.

107. W. A. Mozart, Piano Concerto in D Major, K. 107/1- first movement. Reprinted with permission of the publisher from W.A. Mozart, *Neue Ausgabe sämtlicher Werke,* Serie X, Werkgruppe 28, Abteilung 2 (Kassel: Baerenreiter, 1964).

108. W. A. Mozart, Piano Concerto in E-flat Major, K. 271, first movement. *Neue Mozart Ausgabe* © 1971 Baerenreiter-Verlag. Used by permission.

109. G. B. Pergolesi, *La serva padrona,* part one: Duet: "Lo conosco a quegli ochietti," pp. 53–74. Universal Edition A.G. Wien.

110. Christoph Willibald Gluck, *Alceste*—Act II, scene 3 (excerpt). Reprinted by permission of the publisher from Rudolf Gerber, ed. C. W. Gluck, *Sämtliche Werke,* Abt. I, Bd. 7 (Kassel: Baerenreiter, 1957).

111. W. A. Mozart, *Don Giovanni* (excerpts): Act I, nos. 1–4—Introduction ("Notte e giorno faticar"); Recitative and duet ("Ma qual mai s'offre"); Trio ("Ah! chi mi dice mai"); Aria ("Madamina!").

112. W. A. Mozart, *Requiem,* K. 626—Introit (Requiem), Kyrie.

113. W. A. Mozart, *Die Zauberflöte*: "Der Vogelfänger bin ich ja." © Edwin F. Kalmus. Used by permission.

114. Johann Friedrich Reichardt, *Italien* (Kennst du das Land). © 1964 G. Henle Verlag. München-Duisburg. Used by permission. English translation from Norton Anthology of Western Music by Claude V. Palisca. Copyright © 2001, 1996, 1998, 1980 by W.W. Norton & Company, Inc. Used by permission of W.W. Norton & Company, Inc.

115. William Billings, *Africa.*

116. Edvard Grieg, *Lyrical Pieces,* op. 47: Halling. From Klavierwerke Band I, Lyrische Stücke (Lyric Pieces—Morceaux Lyriques). C.F. Peters.

117. L. van Beethoven, Symphony No. 3 in E-flat Major, Op. 55 ("Eroica"): Allegro con brio; Marcia funebre: Adagio assai.

118. Hector Berlioz, *Symphonie fantastique,* movement 5 (Finale: *Dream of a Witches' Sabbath*).

119. Felix Mendelssohn, *Overture to A Midsummer Night's Dream.* © 1939 Ernst Eulenberg Ltd. © renewed. All rights reserved. Used by permission of European American Music Distributors LLC, sole U.S. and American agent for Ernst Eulenberg Ltd.

120. L. van Beethoven, *Piano* Concerto No. 4 in G Major, Op. 58, 2d movement. Reprinted with permission of G. Henle Publishing from Hans-Werner Küthen, ed., Beethoven Klavierkonzerte II (Munich: G. Henle, © 1996).

121. Beethoven, Piano Sonata No. 21 in C major, Op. 53 ("Waldstein"), first movement.

122. Beethoven, String Quartet in B-flat Major, Op. 130: first movement (Adagio ma non troppo/ Allegro), 2nd movement (Presto), 5th movement (Cavatina: Adagio molto espressivo).

123a. Franz Schubert, *Erlkönig.*

123b. Franz Schubert, *Prometheus.*

123c. Franz Schubert, *Wanderers Nachtlied.*

124a. F. Schubert, *Kennst du das Land*: Mignons Gesang.

124b. Robert Schumann, *Mignon.*

124c. H Wolf, *Mignon II.*

125. Stephen Foster, *Beautiful Dreamer.*

126. Modeste Mussorgsky, *Vchetyrjokh stenakh* ("In Four Walls"), from the song cycle *Bez solnca* ("Sunless"). English translation courtesy of Hyperion Records from Mussorgsky Songs and Dances of Death. Copyright © 1995 by G Schirmer, Inc. (ASCAP). International copyright secured. All rights reserved.

127. Fanny Mendelssohn Hensel, *Trio in D minor,* op. 11, third movement—*Lied.* Hildegard Publishing Company.

128. Frédéric Chopin, *Mazurka in A minor,* Op. 17, No. 4.

129. Frédéric Chopin, *Preludes,* Op. 28, nos. 1–4.

130. Frédéric Chopin, *Ballade No. 1 in G minor,* Op. 23.

131. Franz Liszt, *Galop de bal.* Reprinted with permission from Franz Liszt, *Tänze, Märsche und Scherzi I.* (Budapest: Editio Musica, 1985).

132. Robert Schumann, Carnaval, Op. 9 (excerpts) Papillons—A.S.C.H.—S.C.H.A. (Lettres Dansantes)—Chiarina—Chopin—Estrella.

133. Franz Liszt, *Nuages gris.*

134. Niccolo Paganini, *Caprices,* Op. 1, no. 24.

135. Franz Liszt, *Transcendental Etudes,* No. 1, Preludio.

136. Louis Moreau Gottschalk, *The Banjo.*

137. Giacchino Rossini, *Il Barbiere di Siviglia* (excerpts) Act I, sc. 2 ("Largo al factotum"); Act I, sc. 5 ("Una voce poco fa"). Reprinted with permission of the publisher from Albert Zedda, ed. Giaoacchino Rossini, The Barber of Seville. English version of George Mead (Milano: Ricordi, 1973).

138. Giuseppe Verdi, Rigoletto (excerpts) 1. Act I, Prelude and Introduction—20. Act I, Scene and Duet ("Pari siamo!") Act III, Quartet ("Un dì, se be rammentomi"). English translation reprinted from *The Book of 101 Opera Librettos: Complete English Language Texts with English Translations,* edited by Jessica M. MacMurray.

with plot summaries by Allison Brewster Franzetti. NY: Black Dog & Leventhal Publishers. Copyright © Black Dog & Leventhal Publishers Inc.

139. Richard Wagner, *Tristan und Isolde:* Prelude and excerpt: Act II, sc. 1 (ending)-Act II, sc. 2 (beginning).

140. Sir William S. Gilbert and Sir Arthur Sullivan, *The Pirates of Penzance* (excerpts) Act I, no. 12 ("Hold, Monsters!")— Act I, no. 13 ("I am the very model").

141. Clara Wieck Schumann, *Vorwärts!*. From *Drei gemischte Chöre,* ed. Gerd Nauhaus (Wiesbaden: Breitkopf & Härtel, 1989).

142. Anton Bruckner, *Virga Jesse floruit.* Reprinted by kind permission of the copyright owner. © 1956 by Ludwig Doblinger (B. Herzmansky) KG, Vienna-Munich. English translation MEB.

143. Johann Strauss Jr., *An der schönen blauen Donau (On the Beautiful Blue Danube).*

144. John Philip Sousa, *King Cotton March.* © 1951 The John Church Company. Reprinted by permission.

145. Peter Ilyich Tchaikovsky, *The Nutcracker, Act II* (excerpts) *Le café* (Danse Arabe); *Le thé* (Danse Chinoise); *Trépak* (Danse Russe).

146. Johannes Brahms, Symphony No. 4 in E minor, Op. 98, fourth movement.

147. Antonín Dvořák, Symphony No. 9 in E minor, op. 95 ("From the New World"), Largo, Text and translation: Eulenburg (London) no date, pp. 59-76.

148. Gustav Mahler, Symphony No. 1 in D Major, third movement.

149. Claude Debussy, *Prélude à l'Après-midi d'un faune.*

150. Claude Debussy, *Préludes,* Book 1: Voiles.

151. Béla Bartók, *Mikrokosmos,* Book 4, no. 101: Diminished Fifth. © Copyright 1940 by Hawkes & Son (London) Ltd. Copyright renewed. Definitive corrected edition © copyright 1987 by Hawkes & Son (London) Ltd. Used by permission of Boosey & Hawkes, Inc.

152. Charles Ives, *The Cage.* Words and Music by Charles Ives. Copyright © 1955 by Peer International Corporation. Copyright renewed. This arrangement Copyright © 2009 by Peer International Corporation. International Copyright secured. All Rights Reserved.

153. Charles Ives, *The Things Our Fathers Loved.* Words and Music by Charles Ives. Copyright © 1955 by Peer International Corporation. Copyright renewed. This arrangement Copyright © 2009 by Peer International Corporation. International copyright secured. All rights reserved.

154. Charles Ives, *The Unanswered Question.* Words and Music by Charles Ives. Copyright © 1953 by Peer International Corp. Copyright renewed. This arrangement Copyright © 2009 by Peer International Corporation. International Copyright Secured. All Rights Reserved.

155. Igor Stravinsky, *Le Sacre du printemps,* excerpt from Part 1, *Adoration of the Earth:Introduction, The Augurs of Spring-Dances of the Young Girls.* Boosey & Hawkes, Inc. © 1912, 1921 by Hawkes & Son (London) Ltd. Copyright renewed.

156. Béla Bartók, *Mikrokosmos,* Book 6, no.148: *Six Dances in Bulgarian Rhythm, no. 1.* © 1940 by Hawkes & Sons (London). Copyright renewed. Definitive corrected edition © Copyright 1987 by Hawkes & Sons (London) Ltd. Used by permission of Boosey & Hawkes, Inc.

157. Prokofiev, Piano Sonata No. 7, Op. 83, pp. 24–32. Leeds Music Corp.

158. Darius Milhaud, *Saudades do Brazil* (excerpts) No. 5 ("Ipanema") No. 6 ("Gavea"). © 1922 ℗ 1950 Editions Max Eschig. All rights for the U.S. on behalf of Editions Max Eschig administered by BMG Songs. Inc. (ASCAP). Reprinted by permission of the publishers.

159. Henry Cowell, *The Banshee.* Copyright © 1930 (renewed) by Associated Music Publishers, Inc. (BMI). International copyright secured. All rights reserved. Reprinted by permission.

160. Arnold Schoenberg, *Pierrot lunaire* (excerpts), No. 7 ("Der kranke Mond") No. 14 ("Die Kreuze") No. 21 ("O alter Duft"). English translation by Mimmi Fulmer and Ric Merritt. Used by permission.

161. Anton Webern, *Five Pieces for String Quartet,* Op. 5, No. 4.

162. Alban Berg, *Wozzeck,* Act I, sc. 1—Act I, scene 1. © 1931 by Universal Edition A.G., Vienna © renewed. All rights reserved. Used by permission of European American Music Distributors LLC, U.S. and Canadian agent for Universal Edition. English translation copyright © 1952 by Alfred A. Kalmus, London.

163. Arnold Schoenberg, *Piano Suite,* Op. 25 (excerpts) Praeludium, Menuett. Used by permission of Belmont Music Publishing, Pacific Palisades, CA 90272. Vienna: Universal Edition © 1925.

164. Alban Berg, *Lyric Suite,* third movement (Allegro misterioso). © 1927 by Universal Edition A.G., Vienna © renewed. All rights reserved. Used by permission of European American Music Distributors LL, sole U.S. and Canadian agent for Universal Edition.

165. Sergei Prokofiev, *Classical Symphony,* Op. 25, third movement "Gavotta." Edition A.G., Vienna © renewed. All rights reserved. Used by permission of European American Music Distributors.

166. Kurt Weill, *Aufstieg und Fall der Stadt Mahagonny* ("Alabama Song"). Music by Kurt Weill, lyrics by Bertolt Brecht. Music © 1928 European American Music Corp © renewed. Lyrics © 1928 Stefan Brecht © renewed. All rights for the music outside of the US, Great Britain and the British reversionary territories controlled by Universal Edition A.G., Vienna. All rights for the lyrics outside of the US controlled by Universal Edition A.G., Vienna. All rights reserved. Used by permission of European American Music Corp.

167. Béla Bartók, *Music for Strings, Percussion, and Celesta,* third movement. © Copyright 1937 in the U.S. by Boosey & Hawkes, Inc. Copyright renewed. Used by permission.

168. Sergei Prokofiev, *Alexander Nevsky,* Op. 78, No. 4, "Vstavaite, ludi russkie" ("Arise, People of Russia"). Sobranie Sochinenii, vol. 16A (Moscow: Muzyka, 1965), pp. 38–51

169a. William H. Stepp, *Bonaparte's Retreat.*

169b. Aaron Copland, Four Dance Episodes from *Rodeo*—IV "Hoe-Down" and "Hoe-Down" solo version. Copyright © 1946 in U.S.A. by Hawkes & Son (London) Ltd. Copyright for all countries. All rights reserved.

170. Olivier Messiaen, *Quatuor pour la fin du temps,* First movement (Liturgie de crystal). © 1942 Editions Durand. All rights for the U.S. OBO Editions Durand administeredby BMG Songs, Inc. (ASCAP). Reprinted by permission.

171. Dmitri Shostakovich, String Quartet No. 8, third movement (Allegretto). Copyright © 1953 (renewed) by G. Schirmer, Inc. (ASCAP). International copyright secured. All rights reserved. Reprinted by permission.

172. Thomas "Fats" Waller, *Ain't Misbehavin.*' Words by Andy Razaf. Music by Thomas "Fats" Walker and Harry Brooks. Copyright © 1929 by Mills Music, Inc. Copyright renewed. Assigned to Mills Music, Inc., Chappell & Co. and Razaf Music Co. in the US. This arrangement Copyright 2009 Mills Music, Inc., Chappell & Co. and Razaf Music Co. International Copyright Secured. All Rights Resereved.

173. Leonard Bernstein, "Tonight" from *West Side Story.* © Copyright 1956, 1957, 1958, 1959 by Amberson Holdings LLC and Stephen Sondheim. Copyright renewed. Leonard Bernstein Music Publishing Company, LLC, publisher. Boosey & Hawkes, Inc., sole agent. Used by permission.

174. Benjamin Britten, *War Requiem*: "Let us sleep now—Requiem aeternam—requiescat." © 1962 by Boosey & Hawkes Music Publishers Ltd. German translation © 1963 by Boosey & Hawkes Music Publishers Ltd.

175. Krzysztof Penderecki, *Threnody for the Victims of Hiroshima.* © 1961 (Renewed 1989) EMI Deshon Music Inc. and PWM Editions. All rights reserved. Used by permission. Warner Bros. Publications U.S. Inc., Miami, FL 33014.

176. Ruth Crawford Seeger, *String Quartet* 1931—IV. Finale (Allegro possibile). Copyright © 1941 by Merion Music, Inc. International copyright secured. All rights reserved. Used by permission.

177. Milton Babbitt, *Three Compositions for Piano*, No. 1. © Copyright 1957 by Boelke Bomart, Inc. Used by permission.

178. John Cage, *Our Spring Will Come.* Copyright © 1977 by Henmar Press, Inc. Sole selling agents: C.F. Peters Corporation. International copyright secured. All rights reserved.

179. Hugh Le Caine, *Dripsody.*

180. Terry Riley, *In C* (opening). Published by Ancient Word Music. Administered by Celestial Harmonies. Reprinted by permission.

181. Steve Reich, *Piano Phase* (opening), "Directions for Performance." © 1980 Universal Edition (London) Ltd., London. All rights reserved. Used by permission of European American Music Distributors, LLC, sole U.S. and Canadian agent for Universal Edition.

182. Thea Musgrave, *Orfeo II:* An Improvisation on a Theme (1975). Music by Thea Musgrave. Copyright © 1976 by Novello & Company, Ltd., London, England. All rights for the United States and Canada controlled by G. Schirmer, Inc. (ASCAP). International copyright secured. All rights reserved. Reprinted by permission.

183. Tania León, *A la Par,* Copyright © 1997 by Southern Music Pub. Co. Inc. This arrangement Copyright © 2009 by Southern Music Pub. Co. Inc. International Copyright Secured. All Rights Reserved.

184. Arvo Pärt, *Seven Magnificat Antiphons* © Copyright 1988/1991 by Universal Edition, A.G., Vienna. All rights reserved. Used by permission of European American Music Distributors, LLC, sole U.S. and Canadian agent for Universal Edition.

185. Scott Joplin, *Maple Leaf Rag.*

186. Claude Debussy, *Children's Corner Suite*: "Golliwog's Cakewalk."

187. W.C. Handy, *St. Louis Blues.* Reprinted with the permission of Scribner, an imprint of Simon & Schuster Adult Publishing Group, from Blues: An Anthology by W.C. Handy. Copyright © 1926 by Albert & Charles Boni, Inc. Copyright © 1949 by W.C. Handy and Edward Abbe Niles. Copyright © 1972 by The Macmillan Company. All rights reserved.

188. George Gershwin, *Piano Prelude #2 (Blue Lullaby).* © 1996 Alfred Publishing. All rights reserved. Used by permission.

189. Cole Porter, *Night and Day.* © 1932 (renewed) WB Music Corp. (ASCAP). All rights reserved. Used by permission. Warner Bros. Publications U.S., Inc., Miami, FL 33014.

190. Duke Ellington, *Sophisticated Lady.* Words and Music by Duke Ellington, Irving Mills, and Mitchell Parish. Copyright © 1933 Sony/ATV Music Publishing LLC and EMI Mills Music Inc., in the U.S.A. Copyright Renewed. This arrangement Copyright © 2009 Sony/ATV Music Publishing LLC and EMI Mills Music Inc. in the U.S.A. All rights on behalf of Sony/ATV Music Publishing LLC Administered by Sony/ATV Music Publishing LLC, 8 Music Square West, Nashville, TN 37203. Rights for the world outside the U.S.A. Controlled by EMI Mills Music Inc. (Publishing) and Alfred Publishing Co., Inc. (Print). International Copyright Secured. All Rights Reserved.

191. King Oliver, w/Louis Armstrong: *Snake Rag.*

192. Duke Ellington, "It Don't Mean a Thing (If It Ain't Got that Swing)." Words and Music by Duke Ellington and Irving Mills. Copyright © 1932 Sony/ATV Music Publishing LLC and EMI Mills Music Inc., in the U.S.A. Copyright Renewed. This arrangement Copyright © 2009 Sony/ATV Music Publishing LLC and EMI Mills Music Inc. in the U.S.A. All rights on behalf of Sony/ATV Music Publishing LLC Administered by Sony/ATV Music Publishing LLC, 8 Music Square West, Nashville, TN 37203. Rights for the world outside the U.S.A. Administered by EMI Mills Music Inc. (Publishing) and Alfred Publishing Co., Inc. (Print). International Copyright Secured. All Rights Reserved.

193. Miles Davis, *Blue in Green.* Copyright © 1955 Jazz Horn Music Corp. Copyright Renewed. This Arrangement Copyright © 2009 Jazz Horn Music Corp. All Rights Controlled and Administered by Songs of Universal, Inc. All Rights Reserved. Used by permission.

194. Earl Scruggs, *Foggy Mountain Breakdown.* Copyright © 1950, 1962 by Peer International Corporation. Copyright Renewed. This arrangement © 2009 by Peer International Corporation. International Corpright secured. All Rights Reserved.

195. Chuck Berry, *Roll Over Beethoven.* Words and music by Chuck Berry. Copyright © 1956 by Arc Music Corporation, renewed and assigned to Isalee Music Publishing Co. Copyright renewed by Isalee Music. All rights reserved. Used by permission. International copyright secured.